The GREAT
SPY FILMS

The GREAT
SPY FILMS

by Leonard Rubenstein

The Citadel Press   Secaucus, N.J.

To
Eleanor R. Leon

First edition
Copyright © 1979 by Leonard Rubenstein
All rights reserved
Published by Citadel Press
A division of Lyle Stuart Inc.
120 Enterprise Ave., Secaucus, N.J. 07094
In Canada: George J. McLeod Limited
Don Mills, Ontario
Manufactured in the United States of America by
Halliday Lithograph, West Hanover, Mass.
Designed by William R. Meinhardt

Library of Congress Cataloging in Publication Data
Rubenstein, Leonard.
    The great spy films.
    1.   Spy films — History and criticism.
I.   Title.
PN1995.9.S68R8   791.43'0909'325   79-11563
ISBN 0-8065-0663-6

Acknowledgments

I would like to thank Mark Ricci of the Memory Shop, Ernest Burns of Cinemabilia, Paula Klaw of Movie Star News, Bill Starr of *Film Critic,* Carole Carey of the Museum of Modern Art Stills Archive and William K. Everson for their help in locating the photos with which this book is illustrated. The helpful courtesy of Barbara Humphries and the staff at the Library of Congress made it possible for me to view some of the rarer films I have discussed, while the aid of Paul Myers, David Bartholomew and the other researchers at the Lincoln Center for the Performing Arts Library made it easier to find material on these features. Thanks are also due Barbara Zheutlin and David Talbot for permission to quote from their interview with Albert Maltz. A special debt of gratitude is owed Barbara Lowenstein, Gary Crowdus and Dan Georgakas, who not only had to endure my ravings about the merits of this or that spy film, but also encouraged me to start and finish the book you are about to read.

L.R.

Contents

Introduction

Lurking in the storage rooms of the television networks, the modern film museums and the major distributors are more than 450 spy films that occasionally find their audience at special screenings to honor some director or performer and on late-night television. Many of these films are standardized genre productions with a formula in place of a plot and stereotypes in place of characterizations, but before the formulae were accepted into the studios' canon they had to be tested and proven. Behind the genre and cliché lies a series of inspired images and crafted dialogue in the films this book discusses. Like the actual spies who prepare the ground for invading armies, these fifty films paved the way for hundreds of other, often lesser, films.

Most spy films share a number of elements: suspense, adventure, politics and romance. They may also have certain themes: war, loyalty or paranoia. One set of films may even ridicule the entire art of espionage or, at least, its cinematic complement. The spy films are organized around these topics and themes, but the discussion of them will not avoid the other reality of spy films—that they are reflections of the times and societies which produced them. Just as the real spy is only the tip of an immense and threatening governmental iceberg, the celluloid spy is the created vision of a group of filmmakers: directors, script writers and performers, making an entertainment product for a mass audience. That mass audience, in turn, is influenced by the newspapers it reads, the politicians it elects and the films it sees. Both a reflection and a gauge of popular concerns, the espionage film tells us something about the way we see ourselves in a dangerous, insecure world—the world as we have experienced it, along with the motion pictures, for half a century. A world where hunters and the hunted can never be too sure of the terrain over which they roam nor of their specific roles.

L.R.

1

A Sense of Adventure

Spies
The Scarlet Pimpernel
Pimpernel Smith
The 39 Steps
State Secret
Dr. No
Thunderball
The Ipcress File

Spies have inhabited the borders of recorded history ever since Moses sent agents into the Land of Canaan, and espionage films were among the productions offered a growing audience of moviegoers during World War I. Even before America had entered that war, serials and features touched upon the problem of espionage and personal passion. The American Revolutionary and Civil Wars provided historical settings for the occasional espionage–romance in which the thwarted or threatened love affair had as much, if not more, importance than the actual spying depicted. With the outbreak of war in Europe, Vitagraph, Universal, American Mutual, Fox and Paramount could aim their products at audiences composed, in part, of immigrants from the warring nations. As the war continued, the films began to focus specifically on German agents operating on American soil, rather than placing their heroes and villains in mythical countries and citing unnamed foreign powers. After the United States entered the war in 1917, spies virtually invaded the silent screen as they signalled U-boats off the New England coast, induced German–Americans to work for the Fatherland, attempted to destroy munitions factories and plotted to steal the plans for secret weapons. D. W. Griffith's 1918 feature, *The Great Love,* hinged on the double theme of national and personal betrayal, since the false lover was finally revealed by the heroine as an enemy agent. Since the end of "the war to end war" more than 450 spy films have been made in the United States and Europe. Some of the most famous names in film history have made features with espionage themes and, in many cases, have molded the spy film format. Alfred Hitchcock, Fritz Lang, Anatole Litvak, and Carol Reed are perhaps the most well-known. These filmmakers commented openly on the relationship between the protagonist and the business of espionage, as well as on the conflict between nations that serves as the ultimate struggle in the spy film.

The more immediate struggle, however, was the heroic encounter with overwhelming odds, and the spy protagonist had his first antecedents in the plains cowboy and the urban

11

Kitty (Lien Deyers) studies the photo of her intended victim, Dr. Masimoto. (*Spione*)

detective. Unlike them, the spy's adventures occurred within the larger social or political issues that had immense importance for, and often played an active role in, the film's plot. It was only in an espionage film that an apparent romance could be interrupted by the entrance of the secret police, in fact, where the romance may have been engineered by the secret police. The spy was never a purely lone hero; behind the agent's antics lay a bureaucratic structure of clerks, typists and radio operators whose orders were issued by the same politicians and generals who prepared the armies for the future war the spy was already fighting. The espionage film was the reflection of this reality, sometimes magnified by a filmmaker's vision, occasionally dictated by the same demands that motivated the real spy masters and the citizenry they supposedly protected and, once in a while, formed by an insight into the real drama that lay hidden within the complexities of espionage.

The spy film's first appeal lay in the sense of adventure and suspense it could convey. In many of the best spy films some ordinary screen character was hurled into a situation where bravery and cleverness were needed to stay alive. The more ordinary the protagonist and the more fortuitous the involvement, the more suspenseful the film, since there could be few clues to danger, no signposts to safety. The average person could not rely on secret weapons nor a gymnast's skill, only common sense and wit, and these resources had to be used to survive, to clear one's name of a crime, to save a beautiful woman and/or to avert a national disaster. And when the spy was not at all ordinary, but a beautiful Greta Garbo, or a manly Sean Connery, or a sophisticated Rex Harrison? Then the film clearly beckoned to an audience's image of itself in heroic guise. Suspense could be best served by an ordinary protagonist, but adventure needed a certain amount of glamour and fantasy. Aloof beau-

Haghi (Rudolf Klein-Rogge) confronts his rebellious agent, Sonja (Gerda Maurus). *(Spione)*

ties, brutal multiple murders and bizarre inventions have long been mythic ingredients in the spy film, and still are, although blended in varying degrees according to an audience's changing tastes. The most adventurous spy films could often strain the limits of credulity with impossible technologies and ridiculous plots, but the stakes, even if outrageous to more detached viewers, were clearly recognizable. Patriotic duty, linked to romantic love or sexual conquests, and the trial by ordeal of the hero against armies of evil henchmen completed the fantasy. The spy emerged as a super-hero.

The super-hero, however, required at the very least a nearly equal opponent, and in many spy films the villain played a doubly important role. Besides being a focus of the hero's concern, the villain had his own motivations for evil-doing, whether personal spite or professional status. The "bad guys" also exerted a peculiar charm, since they were the underside to the popular concern with morality. They were allowed to lie and cheat, to disguise their intentions and plot universal domination, while the "good guys" were permitted these luxuries only under special circumstances and for limited periods. The reality of espionage, namely that *all* spies must dissemble and have few scruples, was reserved for only a few early spy films, and since cinematic moral-

ity proclaimed that power itself was wicked, the panoply of grandeur was reserved for and lavished upon the screen villain. Even when the production values—sets, props, costumes and extras—were not too ornate, the villain could be granted a degree of skill and intelligence that a censor would term subversive. Many directors and script writers have created notable antagonists for their films, if only because they have recognized what is apparent to any schoolchild—the more formidable the villain, the more suspenseful the film.

Fritz Lang realized this truth when he made the first serious espionage feature for the Berlin UFA studios in 1928, *Spies (Spione)*. Germany in the late twenties was still recovering from the shocks of defeat and revolution and this could be seen in its films. Spy crazes swept across Europe as rumors of economic catastrophe and revolution were often followed by their actual occurrence. Lang, in an introductory talk for a 1967 screening of *Spies* at the University of California, told the audience that a real incident involving a Soviet trade delegation to London prompted the making of the film and that the villain's (Haghi) makeup was a deliberate allusion to Lenin. Spies had traditionally been seen as unwholesome combinations of the criminal and cunning, so it was natural to give Haghi a distinctly Bolshevik appearance.

A master spy, Haghi is the central focus of *Spies*. He not only controls a small army of dedicated male and female agents, but is also a master of disguise. Within the international banking house that he legitimately heads is hidden an immense headquarters where he briefs his agents and concocts complex schemes against the various government counterspies who try to thwart him. With his black turtleneck sweater and simulated infirmity, Haghi was a classic screen villain, particularly as performed by Rudolf Klein-Rogge, who played Lang's other cinematic villains, Mabuse and Rotwang: Haghi dominated the screen and was introduced by the intertitle card, "Who is at the bottom of all this?" following the theft of important documents and the murder of a foreign diplomat. With his back to the camera, Haghi is shown listening to his agents' reports shown in flashback. Even in this silent feature, Lang's emphasis on realistic detail was evident: one of Haghi's spies gets a copy of an important telegram by placing a pad under one particular counter at the telegraph office and ensuring the use of that counter by breaking the pencils at all the others. Since everyone could appreciate this ploy, Lang had asserted the link between the everyday and the adventurous by depicting one minor trick of the spy's trade. A cross between Bauhaus architecture and a military barracks, Haghi's secret headquarters with its leather-coated messengers, various departments and businesslike atmosphere was also a realistic set.

By contrast, Haghi's foes seem amateurs and bunglers. The secretary to the head of the unnamed nation's secret service is soon revealed as one of Haghi's agents and the film's plot soon develops into a complex match between Haghi's female spies and the counterspies they try to entrap. Romance and sexuality played as much a part in this 1928 film as in any more modern feature film. Haghi's most trusted female agent falls in love with her intended quarry, while the Japanese spy-diplo-

Sir Percy Blakeney (Leslie Howard) amuses the ladies at court by reciting his verse about "that damned, elusive pimpernel." *(The Scarlet Pimpernel)*

Under the wig and behind the false nose is Sir Percy disguised
as a provincial wagonner. *(The Scarlet Pimpernel)*

mat, Dr. Masimoto (Lulu Pick), is not so lucky. His seduction at the hands of Haghi's girlish agent, Kitty, is one of the film's most dramatic moments, since Masimoto has already sacrificed three couriers in a doomed effort to fool Haghi. Faced by his own failure, Masimoto imagines the accusing faces of his drowned couriers shortly before taking his own life in the prescribed ritual. Haghi's defeat occurred not because of his opponents' superior craft but because of romance: his foremost agent had saved the life of the government's top spy. Significantly, Haghi still dominated the film even in the final sequences, when truckloads of armed police sweep into his secret headquarters.

Spies had many elements of the serial to which the early spy film is first cousin. There was a huge cast of characters, almost all of whom are spies for one side or another, a complex series of overlapping plots and an array of mysterious incidents that had Haghi as their focus. His motives for stealing commercial treaties, murdering diplomats and causing economic chaos were kept deliberately vague. A respectable wealthy banker, Haghi seemed to have more than simple avarice in mind as he planned to kill the government's counter-spy. The hint of nihilism or madness in his character was accented by his primary disguise as Nemo, a music-hall clown, the mask behind which he commits suicide when trapped by the police and secret service. In keeping with the melodramatic tradition of the serial, there were few innocent bystanders in *Spies;* all of the major characters are conscious adversaries, and most of the extras as well. When the camera lingers on a street vendor, the audience expects what indeed was to happen—the vendor hurls a bomb at the secret service men, opening the pitched street battle which serves as the film's climax. Whether hero, heroine, villain or madman, all the characters in Lang's film were professional agents.

Spies were seen as mad villains in the twenties, and not only by filmmakers; for decades the rules of war drawn up by conferences in the Hague and at Geneva stipulated that spies could be shot after a requisite investigation and court-martial. In many of the early films and serials, the primary espionage had been committed by enemy agents who were accidentally discovered by the hero or heroine in the course of duty as a reporter, detective or federal officer. Espionage still carried a moral taint, despite the realities of the First World War, and audiences wanted their heroes to *combat,* not *be,* spies. By the mid-1930's, however, the spy's link to heroism and grandeur was reasserted. The Fascist and Nazi seizures of power, as well as the Bolshevik Revolution, meant drastic changes in the European balance of power. Many people in Western Europe and North America were repelled by the new governments they saw emerging in Soviet Russia, Fascist Italy and Nazi Germany, regimes seen as warranting observation by spies. An agent who fought these regimes could warrant an audience's love and admiration. The studios soon found a protagonist in the pages of a popular historical novel set in the period of the French Revolution—*The Scarlet Pimpernel.*

A best-selling novel and successful stage play long before it was filmed in 1935 by Harold Young and Alexander Korda, *The Scarlet Pimpernel* was the Baroness Orczy's revenge upon the French Revolution. The film, like the novel, saw political upheaval and tyranny as the principal foes whose victims, French aristocrats condemned by the Reign of Terror, were saved by a man known only as the Scarlet Pimpernel, from the little English roadside flower left as a calling card. The man was Sir Percival Blakney, Esquire, an apparently ineffectual courtier to the Prince of Wales. As played in the film by the quintessential stage Englishman, Leslie Howard, Sir Percy emerged as a perfect Anglo-Saxon counter to Cyrano de Bergerac. A true dandy who advised the Prince on his choice of clothes and the length of his shirt cuffs, Sir Percy was the last person thought capable of any heroism. The irony of his assumed pose was heightened, in both film and novel, by his having a French-born wife sympathetic to the Revolution's ideals who despised his frivolity.

That Revolution was lent an aura of modern fanaticism by Raymond Massey in the role of Citizen Chauvelin, Ambassador of the First

Richard Hannay (left, Robert Donat), the crofter's wife (Peggy Ashcroft), and the crofter (John Laurie) hear the police at the door. *(The 39 Steps)*

French Republic to the Court of St. James's. Dressed in somber black, a studied contrast to the foppish Percy, Chauvelin was a selfless villain devoted to hunting down the real identity of the Pimpernel. The France depicted in *The Scarlent Pimpernel* was overrun by arrogant soldiers and ruled by murderous fanatics who condemn their enemies to death at Revolutionary Tribunals, travesties of traditional courtrooms. This Victorian image of revolution had ready relevance to Anglo-American audiences in the mid-thirties. The film also had a sub-plot revolving around Sir Percy's brother-in-law, a French Revolutionary moderate who was soon caught up in the internecine political intrigue and must rely on his ostensible opponent, the Pimpernel, to survive. Leslie Howard's Sir Percy could thus be seen not only as a brave humanitarian, but also as a true democrat who would save a revolutionary from the clutches of sectarian rivals.

The Scarlet Pimpernel was curiously free of extensive swordfights or horsemanship, although popular imagination has equated its protagonist with Robin Hood, Cyrano de Bergerac and Captain Blood. It was wit, timing and irony that gave this film its sense of adventure and suspense. The irony of a British aristocrat disguising himself as a harridan gleefully watching the guillotine at work or as an old soldier wearily guarding a road out of Paris gave the film its peculiar charm, just as the frequent, perfectly timed and coordinated escape and rendezvous sequences maintained the suspense. An artfully self-conscious spy, Sir Percy was a heroic amateur who composed silly rhymes about his secret persona to amuse the other courtiers and to allay any suspicions about himself. He also acted out of purely selfless motives, not even patriotism, since England and France were seen as at peace in the film. This setting in a remote, appropriately romanticized period, made it possible to present the Scarlet Pimpernel as a gentleman spy, a master of disguise who was also humane and honorable. In a wartime updating of this character six years later, Leslie Howard produced, directed and starred in *Pimpernel Smith*. Set in Nazi Germany on the eve of the Second World War, Howard played a scholarly, diffident archaeology professor from Oxford who quotes Lewis Carroll in his conversations with Nazi General von Graum (Francis L. Sullivan). The topic of their Shavian dialogue is a mysterious "Mister V" who has spirited a dozen people out of the Gestapo's hands. Professor Smith

Having trusted the Scottish sheriff (left, Frank Cellier), Hannay (right, Robert Donat) finds himself trapped again, but not for long. *(The 39 Steps)*

and Mister V were, of couse, the same man, and the film's delight stemmed from the contrast between Howard, the mild-mannered, efficient humanitarian and Sullivan, the pompous, awkward Gestapo officer.

Other filmmakers during the same period chose to humanize rather than romaticize the spy; for them the major influence could not be the silent serials nor a novel written a decade before the First World War. Heroics and romance had not been part of that war for most of its survivors; that is why the popular imagination had fixated on Lawrence of Arabia and the fighter pilots removed from the banal horror of rats and barrages, lice and poison gas. The average volunteer who had flocked to the recruiters soon realized, if he survived the first few months, that enthusiasm and heroics played little part in a war based on modern industry and mass conscription. On either side of the barbed wire the soldiers saw themselves as victims, fooled by their leaders, sacrificed by their generals and betrayed by their wives. This attitude was carried over into that other

vision of war—the espionage film. The new celluloid spy was not a professional agent, however well intentioned, but a victim cast into a world of intrigue and barely suppressed violence. Audiences could readily identify with this kind of spy, since he, and sometimes she, was an average person—the audience's representative on the screen before it.

This innocent participant in espionage soon learned that a thin line separated normal everyday activity from the mechanics of spying, and this feature became a hallmark of Alfred Hitchcock's early films. Hitchcock's protagonists soon found that decent traits had to be supplanted if they wanted to survive; his amateur agents had to dissemble their aims and to discern the potentially fatal aspects within an apparently harmless situation. This linkage of the terrible with the mundane marked the superb feeling of suspense in Hitchcock's films. The ephemera of daily life was so skillfully blended into the plot of *The 39 Steps* that the novelty of this 1935 film could be gauged only by comparison with *Spies* or

Captured by one of Professor Jordan's men posing as a detective, Hannay (left, Robert Donat) can still joke with another innocent victim, Pamela (Madeleine Carroll). *(The 39 Steps)*

The Scarlet Pimpernel. There were no elaborate disguises with false whiskers and putty noses, only false names and socially acceptable professions to mask the real work of espionage. Hitchcock's villains did not wear the traditional signs, neither distinct foreign accents nor melodramatic cloaks. Pronounced or subtle, their mannerisms indicated the faint clues to their position in the English director's morality tales. And it is a morality tale that his films often resembled, with a naive character introduced to a world of intrigue and terror. Most of his protagonists were more or less forced by circumstances to become spies, and it was assumed by all at the film's end that they would never undertake such work again. In

The 39 Steps the protagonist, Richard Hannay (Robert Donat), found himself embroiled with secret agents and pursued by the English police for a murder he did not commit. Having provided a temporary refuge for Annabella (Lucie Mannheim), a spy whose slight German accent was the only one in the film, Hannay must find her murderers and the secret she was trying to protect.

Unlike the Lang film there was no grandiose plot for domination, just an aircraft engine design that the antagonist had to smuggle out of England. That antagonist, Professor Jordan (Godfrey Tearle), the man with the missing fingertip about whom Annabella has warned Hannay, was simply carrying out a

Hannay (Robert Donat) tries to free himself from his unwilling companion, Pamela (Madeleine Carroll); he succeeds later. *(The 39 Steps)*

A smirking Hannay (Robert Donat) persuades a fearful Pamela (Madeleine Carroll) to join him in his third escape from his foes. (*The 39 Steps*)

standard piece of spycraft. Hitchcock had discovered that the most realistic spies were people who either attracted no undue attention to themselves or so much as to be above suspicion. His villains were not the melodramatic, self-conscious geniuses of a Fritz Lang nor the dedicated fanatics of Young and Korda. They were ordinary people, and, like the hero, usually upper-middle class; they just happened to be enemy agents. Professor Jordan was as determined not to let Hannay's sudden appearance at his home upset his daughter's party as he was to kill him. For his part, Hannay was glad to have found a credulous listener and a refuge from the police, so the quietly dramatic scene in which Hannay realizes that he has delivered himself up to Annabella's foe was a gem of suspense.

Both Hannay and his enemies were intent on doing their jobs with a minimum of bravura and heroics. There was not one serious fist-fight or shoot-out in *The 39 Steps;* Hannay didn't even carry a gun, though he pretends to at one point to insure Pamela's (Madeleine Carrol) cooperation. The film's suspense, as well as its charm, lay in Hannay's use of imagination and good humor to best his opponents, to save his reputation and to protect a military secret. His impromptu speech to an election-

eve audience was one of the film's highlights. While men whom he thinks are the police wait in the wings, Hannay's light bantering with the listeners turns into a heartfelt plea for those who are "lonely and helpless . . . [and] . . . have the whole world against them." Thematically this sequence was an artful reminder of the film's opening in which Mr. Memory (Wylie Watson) exchanged quips with a music hall crowd. This time, however, it allowed for a palatable expression of the light-hearted Hannay's deeper feelings, as well as a delightful expression of wit. As if to underline his joke, Hitchcock's camera showed a captured Hannay acknowledging the audience applause as he is escorted out by the bogus policemen. This speech also marked a turning point in Hannay's journey through the world of deceit and ploy; he had learned, after a few near-fatal errors, to gauge a situation as accurately as possible, to judge people carefully and to take advantage of the slightest opportunity, whether a Salvation Army parade, a political meeting or a friendly inn-keeper. At the film's close, Hannay emerges alive and wiser; he has learned some of the tricks of the seasoned spy without any of the accompanying cynicism or brutality, has learned the secret for which Annabella died and has learned

Having shot Mr. Memory on the stage at the London Palladium, Professor Jordan (Godfrey Tearle) must now try to escape. *(The 39 Steps)*

something about human nature and himself. There was also the literal touch of romance in the final shot of Hannay's hand, complete with dangling handcuff, catching hold of Pamela's.

The setting of *The 39 Steps,* however, was still an insular pre-World War II England, where no one really believed spy stories. As real wars in Ethiopia, Spain and China presaged even wider conflicts, the amateur spy caught by accident in the no-man's-land between rival espionage armies soon disappeared from the screen. The world that emerged after 1945 was shaped by huge standing armies, nuclear weapons and remote-controlled rockets. With the tactics of mass manipulation finely honed by Hitler and Stalin, there seemed little room for the amateur spy. Specially chosen, trained and equipped agents were seen as the only spies able to penetrate the security screens erected

Demonstration in the Vosnian capital honoring the dictator, General Neva (Walter Rilla), upon whom Dr. John Marlowe will unknowingly operate. *(State Secret)*

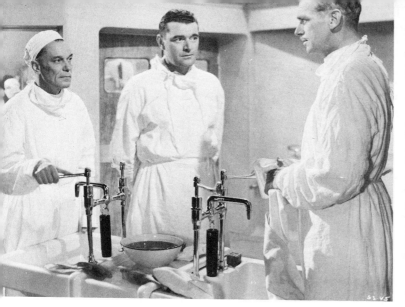

Furious at the attempt to deceive him, Dr. Marlow (right, Douglas Fairbanks, Jr.) confronts both the local surgeon, Dr. Revo (left, Karel Stepanek), and security police head, Colonel Calcon (Jack Hawkins). *(State Secret)*

In this initial test of wits, the American physician Marlowe (left, Douglas Fairbanks, Jr.) has bested the Vosnian colonel, Galcon (Jack Hawkins). *(State Secret)*

by sophisticated technicians on either side of the political barrier thrown across central Europe. Material deprivation and political fear were seen as the hall marks of life in the People's Democracies that arose in the wake of the Red Army's surge towards Berlin. The drabness of life behind the Iron Curtain was featured in authentic backdrops in many spy and suspense films shot in Berlin and Vienna. In many of these films the drabness was incidental to the plot, but one production not only used the drabness of the society as an element in its action but was larded with a gentle irony —the 1950 film *State Secret* (also known as *The Great Manhunt* to late-night television viewers).

Written and produced for Columbia by Sidney Gilliat and Frank Launder, *State Secret* featured the average-man-as-spy theme with Douglas Fairbanks, Jr., as Dr. Marlowe, an American heart surgeon. Lured to a Balkan dictatorship by a series of medical conferences in his honor, Marlowe must operate on the country's ailing dictator. Several days after the operation, the dictator dies, and the film follows Marlowe's efforts to flee the country. At several points in this film a remarkable effect was achieved by the exclusive use of a fabricated language, partially Slavic and Latinate, without any attempt at translation. This device created a fair amount of suspense; there was

Fleeing the police, Marlowe (right, Douglas Fairbanks, Jr.) has spotted a roadblock before he is spotted. *(State Secret)*

Wearing the traditional trench coat, Marlowe (Douglas Fairbanks, Jr.) avoids the fate of the arrested man (center), whom the police suspect of calling the American embassy. *(State Secret)*

constant uncertainty about the correct response to strangers and the real threats that an audience could see in the uniformed political police patrolling the streets in search of Marlowe. The viewers, like Marlowe, had to make reasonable guesses and assumptions. When the surgeon's telephone call to the American Embassy was cut off, the protagonist and audience assumed that the line was controlled by the police. In the next sequence, the police did come to arrest the next person to use that particular public phone, and these scenes used barely two or three lines of English dialogue.

The very drabness and austerity of life in this thinly disguised Eastern European country eventually helped Marlowe. An English-speaking chorus girl (Glynis Johns) looks upon the American doctor as a suitable means by which to leave the country for good. She discusses her desire to leave and shares her rationed supply of cocoa-substitute with him in between bouts of arguments with her roommates about the ownership of a pair of nylons. This unlikely couple soon finds an unlikelier accomplice in Theodor (Herbert Lom), a wealthy smuggler who helps them, if only out of fear. Theodor has to protect his illegal deal-

On their way to flee Vosnia, Lisa (Glynis Johns) and Marlowe (Douglas Fairbanks, Jr.) are the first to leave the cable car. *(State Secret)*

Colonel Galcon (center, Jack Hawkins) galvanizes the officers and men of the border region into action. *(State Secret)*

Only a few yards from the border, Marlowe and Lisa (Douglas Fairbanks, Jr., and Glynis Johns) are surrounded and caught. *(State Secret)*

ings and realizes that no amount of money or influence would protect him from association with a political suspect who reports that the head of state is dead. Both chorus girl and smuggler shared a cynical acceptance of their society and its drawbacks; their dialogue, replete with ironic comments about morality and heroics, was in direct contrast to the film's action.

In a consciously humorous way, the role of the film's major cynic was held by the secret police chief on Marlowe's trail, Colonel Galcon (Jack Hawkins). If the surgeon was an unwilling political fugitive, the head of the nation's security was a detached and affable foe who traded comments on the sham of false democracy and scruples with Marlowe in an opening scene. Galcon, in his position as security chief,

Checking his radioactive equipment, Dr. No (Joseph Wiseman) looks the perfect combination of scientist and scoundrel. *(Dr. No)*

propaganda minister and state secretary, withholds news of the dictator's death, uses a double for ceremonial occasions and mobilizes the secret police to capture Marlowe. The cat-and-mouse game between Galcon and Marlowe comprise the bulk of the film, as a suitably uniformed Minister of the Interior descends upon the rural police to rouse them to apprehend the wanted fugitive.

The emphasis in the escape attempt, despite Fairbanks' reputation for acrobatics and fist-fights, was on imagination, timing and luck, but luck was not completely on the protagonist's side. Not only do Marlowe's guides die, but he and the girl are captured a few hundred yards from the border. Galcon politely and regretfully informs them of their imminent execution, when a radio broadcast of the "dictator's" speech is interrupted by a pistol shot. When Galcon realizes that the double has been assassinated, he also recognizes that Marlowe's importance as a political enemy has vanished. Galcon could pleasantly let them cross the border, but not until the film's writers had one final laugh with their audience. Listening fretfully to the phone report of the assassination, Galcon admits to Marlowe that he is uncertain what his position will be in the new government soon to be formed, whether a fascist, a revolutionary hero or a mere liberal. Turning to Marlowe, the perplexed secret police chief asks him to inquire if there might be a faculty post available in some American college's political science department.

This light-hearted bantering was unusual not only in its setting, a post-war Eastern European dictatorship but also in that the prime vehicle for Gilliat and Launder's humor was a secret policeman. Such a detached view of the Cold War was rare in 1950's spy films; many of these features depicted Soviet spies and Communist agents with many of the conventions once reserved for Nazi spies and saboteurs. The Cold War dominated spy films for nearly a decade; the Soviet Union was seen as the base from and for which whole armies of professional and amateur agents seduced U.S. servicemen, corrupted liberal scientists and stole top secret information. Even an occasional film set in the wartime period might have a subplot indicating Communist intrigue. The easing of the Cold War tensions did not lead to the re-emergence of the witty spy film, but rather to its brutal paradox—light-hearted sadism. Rather than an acceptance of the ideological and human weaknesses that had led to the Cold War, there was an absorption of murderous violence and technical expertise fostered by it. The best cinematic example was Royal Navy Commander James Bond, licensed as 007 by his superiors to kill.

James Bond was the embodiment of pure fantasy; he frequently travels under his own name, making no effort to conceal his identity; his taste for luxury rivals that of any screen voluptuary; he is found irresistible by any number of beautiful women; he is found equally irreplaceable by the London officials he constantly baits, and he disregards both

Despite their submachine guns and Bond's manacles, Dr. No's henchmen are not taking any chances with 007 (Sean Connery) and Honey (Ursula Andress). *(Dr. No)*

common sense and the mathematical odds in his combat with villains whose immense resources and grandiose conspiracies are reminders of Fritz Lang's Haghi. In one crucial area, however, Bond was a realistic spy for his time and audience, since he was basically a sophisticated human adjunct to the technological displays that play so important a part in any Bond films. Suspense in these films lay not so much in the discovery of plots to ruin or rule the world as in the actual machinery of destruction. Although characterized as a cultivated officer and gentleman who knows his wines, paintings and weaponry, Bond must often take a back seat to the super-spy hardware with which he is equipped. Although the first of the Bond films, *Dr. No,* allotted the bulk of its gadgets to the film-title villain (Joseph Wiseman), the later films, in appreciation of audience interest in technology, gave Bond increasing amounts of equipment, too. In the most financially successful of the films to date, *Thunderball,* a back-pack rocket propulsion kit is used peripherally during the precredits sequence and is never seen again.

James Bond (Sean Connery) has eyes only for his ally, Honey (right, Ursula Andress), in this publicity still. *(Dr. No)*

As their emotional addition to espionage, the James Bond films introduced casual sex. The successful seduction of both allied and enemy agents became as much a function of intelligence work as the routine murders committed by both Bond and his various antagonists. As 007, Bond could kill anybody he felt he had to, so that a death that might have been used as a dramatic device in an earlier spy film became part of a sadistic regimen. Even the means of murder had the aura of the grotesque. In *Dr. No,* shortly after Bond has evaded a tarantula dropped onto his bed, he is faced by a human assailant in the bathroom. Bond kills him by flinging the man into the bathtub followed by an electric fan. Bond's dialogue line for the delighted audience? "Shocking." With the exception of *From Russia with Love,* where his opponents were members of the counter-intelligence arm of the KGB, Bond's foes were usually madmen with elaborate facilities and small armies of henchmen. Soon discovered by 007, they are put out of business in a pyrotechnic display of explosions and jujitsu.

There was very little suspense in these films; nobody believed Bond could fail, but there was a childish delight in the shoot-outs, car chases, beautiful women and gimmickry in which the films wallowed. There was also, for more sophisticated tastes, sexual innuendoes-a-plenty in Bond's conversations with the women sent to entrap him. Adventure triumphed over suspense and light-hearted sadism over irony in these films, but they were immensely successful. Perhaps their overstated threats from mad scientists with nuclear weapons factories were a remedy needed by people who had lived for years with atomic air raid alerts and fallout shelter plans. Indeed, the 1960's audience may have been the most appropriate to appreciate the absurdity of megalomaniacs bested by the suave and efficient Bond. Whatever the appeal, the studios reaped large returns from 007, and in the years after 1963 when *Dr. No* was released, producers and their financial backers realized that the big box-office receipts lay where the spies were.

Sean Connery's portrayal of James Bond could be seen as the comic book version of the stage-Englishman updated for an audience that did not remember and might not have appreciated Leslie Howard. Despite a discernible Scotch brogue, Connery had all the marks of elegance attributed to English gentlemen, and he could fight, as well. In 1965 another English spy was sent into the world's movie theaters, Harry Palmer (Michael Caine). Palmer was more akin to the unwilling heroes of Hitchcock's early films than to Lang's. If Bond was an updated aristocrat, Palmer was a contemporary Cockney whose accent contrasted sharply with the Oxford–Cambridge tones of

Production shot of camera crew and soundman during filming of *Dr. No.*

Colonel Ross (Guy Doleman) reminds Palmer of his shady past as well as his current assignment to Major Dalby's department. *(The Ipcress File)*

his superiors whom he loathed, yet had to obey. Although like Bond, Palmer carried a military rank, his was that of a lowly sergeant, and he had been assigned the duties of a spy because Her Majesty's government felt that his talents were wasted in the army prison to which he had been sentenced. Palmer's crime remained vague throughout the three films which feature him as the chief protagonist, but involved a complex fleecing of both the

West German and British armies when he had been stationed in Germany. Although forced into the British Secret Service, Palmer was not a wholly innocent amateur; he was far too good at his job.

The Ipcress File, the first and best of the Harry Palmer films, had as an important focus the rivalry among spies and organizations ostensibly on the same side. While Palmer's superiors (Nigel Green and Guy Doleman) play

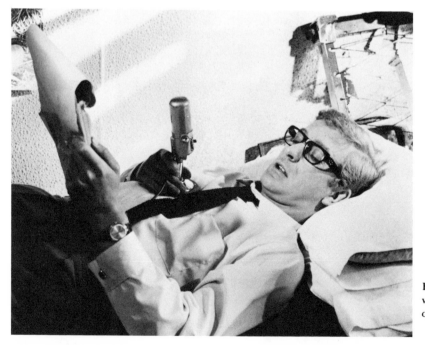

Harry Palmer (Michael Caine) relaxes while recording a report in an early sequence of *The Ipcress File.*

Harry Palmer (left, Michael Caine) has found a better use for the Minox camera Ross (right, Guy Doleman) has given him along with instructions to spy on Dalby. (*The Ipcress File*)

a cat-and-mouse game with each other, Palmer must not only solve the mystery behind the sudden loss of creative talent among a group of government scientists, but must also dodge the CIA agent tailing him. Palmer soon finds the origins of the electronic sounds on a piece of recording tape that is the sole clue to the mysterious "brain drain." Palmer himself is subjected to the behavior modification ma-

chine in a sequence that is one of the film's highlights. A combination sound chamber and multi-sided movie screen, the machine was truly awesome without straining audience credulity. The film's climax showed the interlocking symmetry of the behavior modification theme and the murderous rivalry between espionage chiefs.

Harry Palmer was the logical combination

If teacups could kill, both Major Dalby (left, Nigel Green) and Colonel Ross (Guy Doleman) would be dead. (*The Ipcress File*)

29

During bandshell concert, Nightingale (right, Frank Gatliff) and Dalby (center, Nigel Green) discuss ransom of kidnapped scientist, while Palmer (left, Michael Caine) is visibly distressed by band's rendition of Mozart. *(The Ipcress File)*

of professional and amateur. A curious blend of gourmet and "angry young man," he was an expert spy, in spite of himself. He grudgingly accepted his assignment, baited his superiors, used his imagination to do his job, yet got into a lot more trouble than even he had bargained for. A conscious pawn who wins the understated praise of his superior, Palmer was a character with the dash and vigor to hold audience interest and a sprinkling of realism to satisfy those moviegoers too cynical for

James Bond. Like Bond, however, Palmer was no match for the complex political questions that lie below the surface of the undeclared war. The spy's tricks, his elaborate equipment and the corpses left in his wake did not answer the why's and wherefore's. Those answers lay in political spy films that melded their narratives of individual agents to an allegory of political choices. It was the feel for the political that made the spy film excel.

Harry Palmer (left, Michael Caine) is one of the guards during the ransoming of kidnapped scientist. *(The Ipcress File)*

2

The Feel for Politics

The two Europeans, Teck de Brancovis (left, George Coulouris) and Kurt Muller (right, Paul Lukas), confront each other, while the American family (Donald Woods, Bette Davis, and Lucile Watson) look on. *(Watch on the Rhine)*

Watch on the Rhine
The Iron Curtain
My Son John
Walk East on Beacon
North by Northwest
The Spy Who Came in from the Cold
La Guerre Est Finie
Executive Action

With their mixture of conscious adversaries and innocent amateurs, spy films offered ample room for political nuance and sophisticated intrigue. Rather than merely depict the plight of a protagonist-victim amid espionage's toughened professionals, a filmmaker could show the political strategies and motivations behind their unequal struggle. Since every spy, even the amateur, must learn the tricks of the trade, and every aim, no matter how noble, may involve treachery, the spy film could be both intensely dramatic and political. Whether the politics were made explicitly a part of the action or not, the celluloid spy could be seen as the symbol of the audience's beliefs and sympathies. If Hitchcock had shown moviegoers that spies looked and acted like almost anyone, later filmmakers showed that their motives could be mixed and their politics murky. It was not only spies, counterspies and victims who met in the political spy film, but also all the national loyalties and fears generated by both public and official opinion. An audience's sympathies, like those of the film's characters, could be stretched to

the limit until the climactic revelation of betrayal or fidelity. In its most sophisticated form, the film could not only say something about the protagonist, but more importantly, about the side for which he risked his life. When necessary the political spy films dealt in simple symbols: the protagonist was not only an Everyman, but a specifically American variant; the professionals could be neatly divided between evil foreigners and dedicated federal agents, while the values expressed could be nation and family or rebellion and treachery. In many political spy films made during the 1950's self-righteousness often supplanted any sense of suspense or adventure, let alone reasonable political imagery, and it was a rare film that avoided this failing. Despite flaws, the political spy film broke the confines of the genre with its standardized recourse to foreign accents and caricatured agents, to rooms full of radio equipment and military maps, the detailed explanation of every move and the total avoidance of any thought given to the spy's ultimate purpose and aims. The conscious concerns of both the government and

Anise (Beulah Bondi) and Kurt Miller (Paul Lukas), in *Watch on the Rhine*.

the public could be seen in the political spy film.

The Hal Wallis–Herman Shumlin production of Lillian Hellman's *Watch on the Rhine* appeared in 1943, two years after its original presentation as an award-winning play for officially neutral New York City theater audiences. The film retained the stage play's peacetime setting, but its message had even more relevance for the larger wartime audienece. Sara Muller (Bette Davis) is returning to America with her German husband, Kurt (Paul Lukas), and their three children. Kurt Muller, however, is no ordinary refugee; he had been active in the German opposition to Hitler and had fought in Spain with the International Brigades. The luxurious life in Kurt's mother-in-law's palatial estate outside Wash-

Count Teck de Brancovis (George Coulouris) is not too happy with his wife, Marthe's (Geraldine Fitzgerald), change of heart. *(Watch on the Rhine)*

On the approach to Ottawa's airport, Igor Gouzenko (center, Dana Andrews) gets some final instructions from Colonel Trigorin (left, Frederic Tozere), while a sleepy Major Kulin (Eduard Franz) eavesdrops. *(The Iron Curtain)*

ington, D.C. is a remarkable change for the Mullers after years of poverty-stricken political exile. The daughter of a Supreme Court judge, Sara has to explain to her mother and family retainer that she once did seamstress work to earn money. It is the Muller children who supply the hints about their life in Europe while attracting the attention of a doting grandmother. Kurt finds himself attracting the attention of another house guest and relative by marriage, Teck de Brancovis (George Coulouris). Brancovis, a Romanian aristocrat with a shady past, is a frequent guest at the late night card parties hosted by the German Embassy's military attache.

The film's action develops around several points, some of which have been suggested to the audience in the opening sequences. Sara's mother and brother learn eventually what the audience has probably assumed, that Kurt has no intention of resuming has career as an aircraft designer but has come instead to organize support for his anti-Nazi comrades in Germany. That is why his battered but carefully locked briefcase contains a Luger and $50,000 in cash. Sara silences her mother's protests ("We're all anti-fascists here") with the terse comment that she and Kurt do something about it. The second, more important theme, is the confrontation between the two Europeans, Muller and Brancovis. From their first meeting, Brancovis has been curious about

Embassy Guard Sergeyev (right, John Shay) warns Gouzenko (left, Dana Andrews) about the protection of code books and documents. *(The Iron Curtain)*

The self-possessed Gouzenko (Dana Andrews) is about to tell Karanova (June Havoc) his secret—that he loves his wife. *(The Iron Curtain)*

Kurt, a man with the traces of bullet wounds and torture who has lived in the countries bordering on Nazi Germany. Having discovered Kurt's mission, Brancovis threatens to tell the German Embassy, especially since Kurt has decided to return to Germany illegally. One of his comrades, a man who had once saved his life, has been recently arrested by the Gestapo, and Kurt has resolved to rescue him. While the American relatives go to fetch their checkbooks and household cash to buy Brancovis's silence, Kurt goes to grab for his gun. Kurt had guessed that the Germans would pay the Romanian with a sanctioned return to Bucharest, where with the money he could enjoy the life of "shabby palaces and cafes." Rather than

rely on the day or two of silence that fear might generate, Kurt tells Brancovis that to guarantee his silence and the security of his mission, he must kill him. This confrontation is the best sequence in the film in terms of sheer drama, intelligent dialogue and performance, and Lukas was awarded an Academy Award for his role in *Watch on the Rhine.*

From this encounter Kurt's American in-laws, and ostensibly the audience, learned that different kinds of people helped the Nazis for varied reasons, homesickness and an open dislike of poverty, in Brancovis's case. They also learned the reasoned ruthlessness with which Kurt and Sara have had to act for the past years in order to "do something" about the anti-Nazi cause. Following Brancovis's murder, Kurt leaves for Germany, a trip apparently being traced on a map in the following scene, until we learn that it is Kurt's oldest son planning to take up his father's mission. The implication, of course, is that Kurt has died trying to save his friend.

As portrayed by Paul Lukas, himself an actual refugee from Hitler, Kurt is the idealized characterization of the "good" German, the "premature anti-fascist." Premature because his politics came at least half a decade too soon for public or government opinion in England or America. Adapted for the screen from Hellman's play by Dashiell Hammett, the dialogue had several references to the Spanish Civil War, one within the film's first five minutes, and Sara's comments to her wealthy mother about the work people must

The "good Russian" Gouzenko (left, Dana Andrews) hears Major Kulin's (Eduard Franz) half-drunk confession of disillusionment with Communism. *(The Iron Curtain)*

do to earn a living leave no doubt about the film's left-wing tone. The temper of those times was revealed by Lukas's refusal to appear in the studio when Kurt's on-camera death was to have been filmed. In accord with the morality of the Production Code, Kurt, as the cold-blooded murderer of Brancovis, had to die, so that the implication of his death was added at the film's close. Kurt was shown as a complex character who explains his actions to his American relatives and even raises the possibility that he too has become a murderous political fanatic, "one of the sick of the earth." Hammett's craftsmanship included not only Brancovis's treatment as an apolitical opportunist, but also several German characters, Brancovis's poker partners, who represented German tradition: an aristocratic army officer, and its Nazi debasement, a Gestapo functionary. Kurt, of course, represented the other side of Germany, the broken tradition for freedom and social equality.

Following the war politics again made an entrance into the celluloid cloak and dagger tale, but with an altered perspective. The enemy to be caricatured was not German Fascism, but Soviet Communism. Soviet Russia's conventional military hegemony and west-

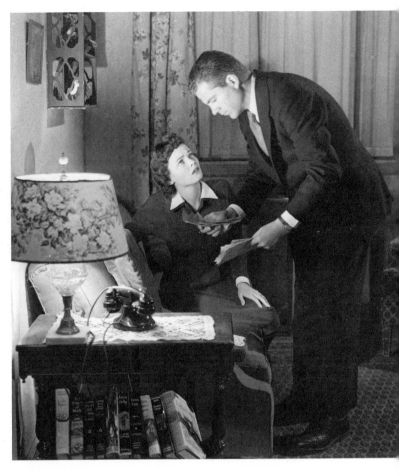

Gouzenko (Dana Andrews) and his wife, Anna (Gene Tierney), assemble the documents with which they plan to defect to the Canadians. *(The Iron Curtain)*

Gouzenko (left, Dana Andrews) tries unsuccessfully to get newspaper editor (Leslie Barrie) to believe his story of Soviet espionage. *(The Iron Curtain)*

NKVD man Ranev (left, Stefan Schnabel) starts to talk Gouzenko (Dana Andrews) into returning to the embassy, while Bushkin (Noel Cravat) and Colonel Trigorin (Frederic Tozere) wait. (*The Iron Curtain*)

ward expansion dominated postwar Europe's map, and the fact that Stalin was a cruel dictator was remembered as quickly as it had been forgotten during the Red Army's fearsome battles with the Wehrmacht. Hollywood's homage to the Soviet war effort could be seen in *Mission to Moscow, North Star* and *Counter-Attack,* while even a mediocre spy film, *Berlin Correspondent,* could have its Gestapo officer threaten his bungling subordinates with transfers to the Eastern Front. The studio atmosphere changed drastically after the war. Not only did films try to explain the expansion of Soviet influence in terms of the melodrama by which they explained the war: fanatics, Fifth Columnists and traitors, but Congressional and private investigations hounded the very writers and performers who might have been able to explain the Cold War with some degree of skill. The espionage films that grew out of the 1950's were, of course, anti-Communist, but there was an interesting variety of approaches. Hollywood mirrored the mixture of rational fear and irrational panic felt towards Communism. The facts were that the Red Army was the world's largest, that Soviet foreign policy was dictated as much by Stalin's will as by Marx's theories, that Communist tactics could be fatally complex even for idealistic

supporters, and that the countries occupied by the Red Army, with the exception of Czechoslovakia, had been fascist allies or notoriously undemocratic long before the war. There was also much that was purely emotional: confusion about decisions made at the conferences at Teheran, Yalta and Potsdam; the popular suspicion of anything novel or eccentric; the fear of critical opinion or thought, and the charge of Communist hurled against anything with explicit social implications. With the exception of Gilliat and Launder's *State Secret* the 1950's spy films began to reflect this ambivalence.

The Iron Curtain and *My Son John* were two spy films that reflect the vacillation between sensible fear and mindless suspicion. Both were made by major studios with major performers within several years of each other. Based on the actual defection of Soviet Embassy code clerk Igor Gouzenko to Canadian officials with information about the spy ring operating out of Ottawa, *The Iron Curtain* used a quasi-documentary style with newsreel clips and a voice-over narration to hammer home its serious theme of Soviet espionage. From its opening credits in plain typescript against a white backdrop, William Wellman's film aims for a documentary effect. There was even a shot of the published Royal Commission report on Soviet spying, and Wellman had used location shooting and a score drawn from Soviet symphonic works to heighten the illusion of a clinically unbiased report.

Igor Gouzenko (Dana Andrews) is pointed out to the audience by the off-screen commentator (Reed Hadley) as he steps off the plane carrying new staff members for the Soviet embassy in Canada. Gouzenko is the only civilian among them, and the embassy has a decided militaristic tone, with lots of uniforms, armed gurads and an aggressive preoccupation with security. When questioned about his training by the NKVD officer, Ranev (Stefan Schnabel), Gouzenko tells him that he has been trained as a code and ciphers clerk by military intelligence and has been assigned duty with the Foreign Ministry. Ranev rebukes him soundly for his honesty, since no one, including embassy colleagues, must know his training nor exact duties. To show the personal effects of this officially bred suspicion, Milton Krims' screenplay had Ranev's secretary, Karanova (June Havoc), attempt the seduction of Gouzenko. In her lavishly furnished apartment Karanova asks him about his job at the embassy, but Gouzenko has not been in Canada long enough to forget his Soviet training nor to be fooled so easily. The only secret he tells her is that he drinks vodka like a true Russian and that he loves his wife. Shortly before leaving her, Gouzenko warns Karanova that if she dares lie about him, he will inform the NKVD officer of her botched attempt to get information. One of the film's major points was to depict the harried, tense life inflicted upon Sovict citizens, and in particular Gouzenko, by tyrannical officials and policemen. At one point he is even denied time off to see his son's birth, since he has to encode and transmit important secret messages from his office hidden in the embassy.

By means of off-screen narration, Gou-

FBI Inspector Stedman (Van Heflin) and Mrs. Jefferson (Helen Hayes) meet "accidentally" on the banks of the Potomac. *(My Son John)*

Lucille Jefferson (Helen Hayes) talks to the family's priest, Father O'Dowd (Frank McHugh). (*My Son John*)

zenko's work is linked to the network of Communist agents and sympathizers who supply the information sent to Moscow. The network is headed by a Canadian Communist named Grubb (Barry Kroeger), who is depicted as imperious enough to tell Ranev angrily that he takes his orders from Moscow, not its embassy. As a known Communist, Grubb is an important character in the film, since he talks mere sympathizers into becoming spies. In one brief meeting, Grubb talks an RCAF officer into getting secret war information for the Party. While lessons in Marxism can be heard from an adjoining room, Grubb tells the officer that there are many kinds of Marxists: talkers, faddists and doers. Grubb flatters the man into aiding Marxism in the most concerte manner, while the pauses in their conversation are filled by Karanova's recitation of the day's lesson in dialectics. The moral was painfully obvious: an interest in Marxism will lead to treachery if the right approach is used, and since no one with any self-esteem would want to be thought of as an idler or poseur, the progression was certain. In a similar scene, Grubb pressures a nuclear scientist into continuing his allegiance to the Soviet Union and to pass on information concerning his work in an effort "to bring peace to the world." These scenes, in gloomy drawing rooms and ill-lit

apartments gave *The Iron Curtain* the claustrophobic menace of the gangster film, while Grubb's arrogant and insinuating voice was a perfect cross of intellectual and thug.

The effects of suspicion and tyranny could be seen in the lives of the embassy staff. One army major (Eduard Franz) drinks himself into a nightly stupor to forget that his father, once a great revolutionary, now makes his living by repeating the government's lies. No one, certainly neither Ranev nor Grubb, is shown as a revolutionary, but rather as functionaries with varying degrees of authority and power. Igor, referred to by the commentator and some of the other characters as a simple Russian, was the film's only hero. With his life bounded by the demands of war and work, Igor has to remind his wife not to be too friendly with her Canadian neighbors, and one sequence shows the Gouzenkos walking past a church one spring day with sad averted eyes, while the sound track carries the parishioners' hymn. Igor's few pleasures stem from his marriage and his wife's pregnancy, yet even that pleasure is denied him when he must radio reports on the atomic bomb research to Moscow on the day of his son's birth. The atomic bomb meant peace to a war-weary nation, as shown in newsreel shots of jubilant crowds, but in the basement of the Soviet em-

The FBI agent (Van Heflin) and the traitorous son, John (Robert Walker), vie for Lucille Jefferson's (Helen Hayes) allegiance. (My Son John)

bassy a different kind of crowd has gathered. Flanked by portraits of Lenin and Stalin, Ranev in full-dress uniform tells a huge audience, apparently the province's entire contingent of sympathizers and agents, that the class struggle and relentless realism must continue. In the dimly lit hall, the ruthless Ranev must have been Wellman's idea of the "comrade commissar" rousing his operatives to bigger and better conspiracies. Igor, however, soon has reason to engage in his own private intrigue.

Fearing their imminent return to Russia, Igor and his wife peer at their infant son, and her comment that no human being should live in fear prompts his action. Gradually he steals secret information from his files, and one morning goes with his family to the Canadian Ministry of Justice rather than to the Soviet embassy. Fearful that Grubb may have agents on the ministry staff, Igor insists on seeing the Minister, a demand that is not met. Bad luck also greets the Gouzenkos at the office of the capital's newspaper where the editor dismisses his revelations as a lunatic's ravings. By evening, an anxious Gouzenko sends his wife and child to stay with a neighbor, while Ranev and Grubb calculate the chances of their spy network surviving Gouzenko's defection. It is during this discussion that Grubb confidently

suggests that unless Gouzenko has found a Canadian refuge, he could very well be at home. Ranev and two army officers confront Gouzenko, who is about to give himself up to them, when like a deus ex machina the Royal Canadian Mounted Police comes to the rescue. Summoned by the neighbor, the Canadian constable cleverly uses Ranev's claim to be retrieving stolen embassy material from a delinquent employee to trap the NKVD official. Glancing from Ranev to the terrified Gouzenko family, the constable demands that, in accordance with the law, Ranev must identify the stolen material at the RCMP headquarters. Ranev, of course, cannot, and the subsequent series of scenes depict the arrest and trial of the various Soviet spies we've seen in the film. One of the indicted agents, a Canadian parliamentarian, appeals for help to Grubb, who returns with the airy promise to name a city after him when they take power. This cynical comment, an indication of the real contempt Communists have for their minions and a reflection on the Soviet practice of naming cities after martyred revolutionaries and political bosses, was followed by a last look at the Gouzenko family, the simple Russians. Shepherded by RCMP plainclothesmen, they are seen walking towards a hillside home on the rural farm where, we are told by the

41

Millie (Virginia Gilmore) and Alex (Karel Stepanek) examine the microfilm of secret documents in this visual cliché. *(Walk East on Beacon)*

narrator, they live under an assumed name.

Although murky about the actual motives and mechanics of the spies involved, *The Iron Curtain* was based on a real enough defection and actual espionage activities. Ranev and Grubb were, of course, the Cold War stereotypes of Soviet policeman and Communist Party organizer; both were cynical, Grubb perhaps even more than Ranev, ruthless, ty-

rannical and cunning. Neither had a doubt about their goals nor any illusions about methods. Gouzenko, "the simple Russian," defected for purely personal reasons, not because of any selfless political reasons. Typically, the only self-conscious character was the revolutionary's son, and he is cast as an alcoholic fearful of his own wife, a comic rather than tragic figure, despite his tearful admission that he had executed several men in order to glean volunteers for a perilous frontline mission. Because the film lacked a fanatic and *idealistic* Communist character, even in terms of the traditional screen villain with near-mad ambitions, *The Iron Curtain* has a somewhat flat tone, in keeping with its quasi-documentary style, that keeps audience emotions at a comfortable distance. Another Cold War film without such distance was *My Son John.*

Made in 1952, Leo McCarey's production did not even deal with a fabricated case of espionage, but was a startling proof of the contemporary obsession with Communists as potential spies lurking within the federal government. Since it embodied many of the features of the witch-hunting mentality, *My Son John* has become a classic of the McCarthy era. The film opens with a suburban tree-lined street in which two young men in army uniforms are playing football. The two soldiers are the Jefferson brothers home for a send-off

A seated Alex (Karel Stepanek) shows his unsuccessful predecessor, Martin (Ernest Graves), the cost of failure in the spy war. *(Walk East on Beacon)*

party prior to their embarkation for the fighting in Korea. Headed by Lucille (Helen Hayes) and Dan (Dean Jagger), the Jefferson dinner party is missing one member, the oldest son, John (Robert Walker). When John calls to announce that he has been delayed, there is a fair amount of sniggering on the part of his father and two brothers about John's use of "two-dollar words" and his high government position, while Lucille sticks up for her obvious favorite. When John finally does arrive, the tension between father and son is readily apparent. The young man laughs off his schoolteacher father's patriotism and avoids his direct question as to whether he is "one of those Commies" about whom the father has learned at American Legion meetings. John not only ignores his parents' devotion to religion but makes a point of subtly insulting the local priest. This intellectual arrogance is also linked to a genuine snobbery; he prefers visiting an old college instructor to being with his parents and, in one painful scene, tries to engage the family physician in a discussion by appealing to him as "a man of science." The implications of this characterization were bluntly apparent; just as they belittled their parents skeptical intellectuals had a tendency to treason. The link made in this film between love of parents and love of country overwhelmed its espionage motif to such an extent that *My Son John* was as much an Oedipal as a Cold War morality tale.

Lucille Jefferson, who had taken a phone message for John from a woman who refused to leave her name, was the film's fulcrum. John has told her that he had no women friends in Washington, so that his mother begins to have suspicions. Her fears are augmented by the arrival of FBI agent Stedman (Van Heflin), who tells Lucille that John is being investigated in connection with a known Communist spy, a woman named Ruth Carlin (Irene Winston). Stedman senses that John's mother is the only person who could connect him with Carlin. She could; not only had she received the phone call, but she found a key in a torn pair of trousers John had left with her to donate to the church rummage sale. Lucille journeyed to Washington by plane to return

FBI Inspector Belden (George Murphy) and one of his agents examine the microfilm they have snatched from the enemy spies. *(Walk East on Beacon)*

the trousers, and she grimly noticed how he felt for the missing key while glibly discussing the ease of repairing the rip. Tormented by doubts, Lucille meets Stedman on a park bench in a chance encounter staged by the FBI. Followed by other FBI agents, Lucille goes to the Carlin apartment where the key she has taken from the trousers' lining opens the door.

Stedman has now won the psychological spoils; Lucille Jefferson realizes that her favorite son is a spy, or at least implicated in espionage activities. As a result of this unwanted revelation, she suffers a nervous breakdown, and even John begins to waver in his earlier decision to evade arrest by flying to Lisbon. While on his way to surrender to Stedman, John's cab is machine-gunned near the steps of the Lincoln Memorial, but a tape-recorded confession he has made shortly before his murder is played to a graduating class as a warning to them about the dangers of Communism. His warning goes so far as to mention "the eyes of Soviet agents that are even now upon you." The beams of light, the uplifted faces and the inspirational music heightened the religious tone of the scene. John has redeemed his soul through confession and death, while the closing scene of Lucille and Dan Jefferson going to church to pray for his soul reinforced this religiosity.

My Son John used the theme of espionage to underline the dangers posed by Communist subversion to the family and domestic life. John had lied to his mother about his politics, claiming to be a liberal, had gotten into a fight with his father about the Bible and had demonstrated his aversion to the family priest. As if this behavior were not suspect enough, he is contrasted with two younger brothers facing the Communist foe in Korea. John's own father had guessed that he was indeed a Communist, and that most potent paternal figure, the FBI, had already prepared a dossier on him and, in the form of Stedman, was closing in for the arrest. The film mentioned no secret formulae or missing documents; there were no coded messages nor radio transmissions, and there wasn't even a direct mention of John's actual government job. Freud seemed to have been more the inspiration for *My Son John* than Joe Stalin, since John's characterization was more of a homosexual intellectual than a Communist spy. The almost carica-tured attention lavished by John on his mother, his indifference to women, his dislike of his father and general manner supported this interpretation. Seen at a distance of twenty-five years, Lucille's anguish over finding a woman's apartment key in her son's pants might have had nothing to do with Communist subversion, the FBI or the Korean War.

Freudian clichés and emotional caricatures had nothing to do with another anti-Communist spy feature made in the same year, *Walk East on Beacon.* If *My Son John* indicated the irrational tone of the Cold War, *Walk East on Beacon* tried for the semblance of reality attempted in the earlier *Iron Curtain.* Producer Louis de Rochemont had pioneered the quasi-documentary spy film in America; his *House on 92nd Street* had been a great commercial and critical success.

In *Walk East on Beacon* director Alfred Werker used stock footage scenes of FBI investigative techniques to protray the successful penetration of a Soviet spy ring in the Northeast. Based unabashedly on a published report by FBI Director J. Edgar Hoover, the

Inspector Belden (George Murphy) about to relay orders to his team of FBI men, played in most part by actual FBI agents. *(Walk East on Beacon)*

film lost few opportunities to depict the means by which East European Communists controlled their American agents. One of these spies, Martin (Ernest Graves), is kidnapped and bustled aboard a Polish freighter, both to pay for his failure and to make room for a more expert spy imported from Europe. The purpose of all this espionage activity was the acquisition of scientific information concerning a Project Falcon, the plan to put a space station into orbit around the earth—the ultimate weapon, a voice-over warned the audience. The information came from one of the project's scientists who was fearful for his son, a captive in East Germany. Since few of the Americans were dedicated Communists, the FBI's task was to save Martin, keep track of his replacement, Alex (Karel Stepanek), and supply false information to preserve the spy network for the sake of the scientist's son. A tall order, indeed!

By means of secret cameras, lip readers and even a television camera, FBI Inspector Belden (George Murphy) kept track of the Red spy ring which stretched from Boston to Washington. Location shooting gave the film a veneer of realism, as did the use of actual FBI men grouped around Belden's desk receiving their daily instructions and explanations for the day's events. Since the emphasis was on the technical details of surveillance and capture rather than on character or motives, this quasi-documentary had many of the same flaws as *The Iron Curtain,* graphic but lifeless, realistic but flat, portentous but conventional.

There were other films, such as *Big Jim McClain* and *Pick-up on South Street,* that bordered on self-parody with thin intrigues and overly violent flag waving. Few truly powerful anti-Communist spy films emerged from Hollywood, perhaps for the same reasons that there were so few about the Korean War during the same period. Creative energy went instead into spy films set in the Second World War. Many of these "now-it-can-be-told" films were produced on location with European supporting casts for a fraction of the normal studio cost. The anti-Communist spy dramas

The scientists working on Project Falcon, over which the Communist and FBI agents waged their secret war. *(Walk East on Beacon)*

were notoriously serious; entertainment suffered from a devotion to political morality, but one famous filmmaker, Alfred Hitchcock, did make a humorous feature about the Cold War.

Hitchcock's 1959 feature, *North by Northwest,* could be seen as the cinematic armistice ending the worst phase of the Cold War. Soviet-American rivalry was used by Hitchcock and his script writer, Ernest Lehman, to experiment with the familiar theme of the innocent bystander caught in the cross-fire of spies and counterspies. The hero-victim in this film was Roger Thornhill (Cary Grant), a New York City advertising excutive who, in order to avoid his mother, uses a phony name at a hotel luncheon. Responding to a message for him under his assumed name, George Kaplan, Thornhill is whisked away at gunpoint to a palatial estate where he is questioned about CIA activities by a Phillip Vandamm (James Mason), who appeals to him as "one professional to another." Thornhill's refusal to admit his "real" identity is taken as opposition and he is left drunk in a car aimed at a twisting cliffside road. The would-be victim of an auto accident, Thornhill manages to drive himself into arrest on the charge of drunk driving. The police naturally refuse to believe his story of abduction, espionage and attempted murder, but release him with a warning and, to add insult to injury, in the custody of his mother. Frustrated by their incredulity,

Mistaken for the "other" George Kaplan, Roger Thornhill (center, Cary Grant) realizes he is being kidnapped by Licht (left, Robert Ellenstein) and Valerian (Adam Williams). *(North by Northwest)*

Thornhill returns to the hotel to investigate the actual George Kaplan paged by the hotel clerk the day before. A George Kaplan was, of course, duly registered and his hotel room was suitably furnished with luggage, clothes and even a few phone messages. In his effort to find the reason for his abduction, Thornhill even accepts a telegram addressed to Kaplan, but his quest is motivated more by vanity than by fear. Thornhill resents the idea that the police, his mother and friends think he had

Plotting the enemy's movements by radio was one of the technical improvements in modern espionage featured in *Walk East on Beacon;* Inspector Belden (George Murphy) hovers over the radio operator.

Spy master Phillip Vandamm (James Mason) reads an incredulous Thornhill (center, Cary Grant) a list of his movements as George Kaplan. *(North by Northwest)*

Licht (foreground, Robert Ellenstein) and Valerian (Adam Williams) prepare Roger Thornhill (Cary Grant) for his death ride. *(North by Northwest)*

made up the story of spies and murder to account for his drinking. That motivation changes abruptly, however, when a second assassination attempt fails, but implicates Thornhill in the knifing of a featured UN speaker.

The similarity to *The 39 Steps* was obvious, but *North by Northwest* focused, as well, on the actual manipulation by the spy masters and not only the antics of their pawns. Seated at a conference table, the Professor (Leo G. Carroll) tells his CIA intelligence staff that their nonexistent decoy, Kaplan, has turned into a live decoy, Thornhill. One of the spy masters responds by noting that the whole situation is so sad that he feels like laughing. The only way to protect Thornhill, the Professor notes, is to have him protected by the double-agent already working with Vandamm. In a sly understatement, the CIA Professor adds that to protect the live decoy the threat to their agent would be too dangerous by far.

Hunted by spies as George Kaplan, and now wanted by the police as Roger Thornhill, the hapless executive is forced to discover the identity of George Kaplan in order to solve his singular dilemma. Thorhill's honest confusion is heightened by meeting Eve Kendall (Eva Marie Saint) on a train heading for the Southwest. She willingly helps him, while both the dialogue and visual imagery (the train entering a tunnel) hint at a sophisticated flirtation. The flat-lands of the American Midwest became the site for one of Hitchcock's most famous sequences. Lured to a rural highway intersection by a meeting with the mysterious Kaplan, Thornhill finds himself the lone victim of a strafing attack by a crop-dusting aircraft. Having survived this third attempt on his life, Thornhill then seeks out Eve, only to be shocked by finding her at an antiques auction in the company of Vandamm. The victim-protagonist eludes one more trap by staging an unpleasant scene (he bids an enormous sum for an antique) and being escorted away by the local police. Rather than placing him under arrest, however, the cops deliver him into the hands of the Professor. Informing him of Eve's true role as a double-agent and that he has endangered her, the Professor, neatly attired with fedora and cane, talks Thornhill into aiding the CIA plan to arrest Vandamm before he can leave the country

Thornhill (Cary Grant) discovers the knife hurled into the back of Lester Townsend (Philip Ober) by a fleeing Valerian in the UN lobby. *(North by Northwest)*

with valuable information. This information was never explained: it was the famous Hitchcockian "MacGuffin"—the plot device around which spies, counterspies and protagonists plot and scheme.

Thornhill (Cary Grant) crawls out from under the front end of the fuel truck into which the crop duster piloted by Licht has crashed. *(North by Northwest)*

Eve Kendall (Eva Marie Saint) "shoots" Thornhill (Cary Grant) before Vandamm (right, James Mason) or Leonard (far right, Martin Landau) can stop her. *(North by Northwest)*

The balance between comedy and drama, always a delicate one in Hitchcock's films, neared the burlesque in a spy film with an ostensible Cold War theme. Although Vandamm's subordinate, Leonard (Martin Landau), was a somewhat grim figure, both senior spy masters were coolly professional characters. Neither made any speeches about patriotism or class struggle, and the Professor helped Thornhill only because his own plans had been endangered. As played by Grant, Thornhill was a light-hearted figure, an urbane Richard Hannay, who unthinkingly took on the burdens of espionage for selfish reasons. *North by Northwest* was a watershed; few films after it could treat domestic espionage

Eve Kendall (Eva Marie Saint) sees one last hope for escape from Vandamm (left, James Mason) and his henchmen, Valerian (Adam Williams) and Leonard (Martin Landau). *(North by Northwest)*

49

with half the gravity formerly accorded it. Gun play, car chases and plans for world conquest were the preserve of James Bond, and few directors tried to raise the specter of Soviet spies in the midst of a middle-class America with any of the melodrama of *My Son John* or *Walk East on Beacon*. Although Hitchcock did film a joke about an advertising executive become CIA decoy, he did not satirize the basic premise of the quiet war between spies and counterspies. Vandamm did have secret information, vague as it was, and showed little remorse about the murders committed by his henchmen. In 1965, however, a cinematic attack on the basic foundation of Cold War espionage did appear, *The Spy Who Came in from the Cold*.

Based upon a successful novel by John Le Carré, the film version detailed the "disagreeable things . . . occasionally very wicked things" that spies must do to safeguard national defense. Directed by Martin Ritt, one of the filmmakers blacklisted during the 1950's, *The Spy Who Came in from the Cold* displayed a carefully honed feeling for politics unseen in American spy films since *Watch on the Rhine*.

Eve Kendall (Eva Marie Saint) demonstrates the properly romantic counterspy's attitude toward Thornhill (Cary Grant) in this publicity still. *(North by Northwest)*

Leamas' agent (Karl Riemeck) shot down while leaving East Berlin in film's opening. *(The Spy Who Came in from the Cold)*

At the small library to which he has been assigned as cover, Leamas (Richard Burton) meets assistant librarian Nan Perry (Claire Bloom). *(The Spy Who Came in from the Cold)*

Paul Dehn's screenplay, like the Le Carré novel, had its strength in a scheme that was only partially revealed to audience and protagonist alike. The protagonist, Alec Leamas (Richard Burton), was a combination of professional and victim, since he only realized the Machiavellian quality of his assignment at the end. A seasoned veteran of the spy war, Leamas had few illusions and scruples, yet was himself shocked by the ruthlessness of his superiors in London. This film also had something unusual for any spy film—an enemy agent, Fiedler (Oskar Werner), whose appeal

Alec Leamas (Richard Burton) will soon learn that Nan Perry (Claire Bloom) is a member of the English Communist Party. *(The Spy Who Came in from the Cold)*

George Smiley (right, Rupert Davies) looks on while Alec Leamas (Richard Burton) receives instructions from his control (Cyril Cusack). *(The Spy Who Came in from the Cold)*

51

An adoring Nan (Claire Bloom) accompanies an embittered Alec (Richard Burton) from Wormwood Scrubs Prison. *(The Spy Who Came in from the Cold)*

A waiting Fiedler (center, Oskar Werner) asks the seated escort officer for the report on the defector Leamas (Richard Burton). *(The Spy Who Came in from the Cold)*

Fiedler (background, Oskar Werner) explains to Leamas (Richard Burton) that he is the cheapest currency of the Cold War and that no one will mourn his death. *(The Spy Who Came in from the Cold)*

to both audience and Leamas alike was part of the film's artistry.

As the control and major contact for British agents in East Germany, Leamas had developed a hatred for a man he had never met or seen, the head of East German Counter-

Intelligence, Mundt (Peter Van Eyck). Leamas has agreed to pose as a defector to pass on just enough information to implicate Mundt as a traitor, a double-agent working for the British. Leamas was to play the role of a catalyst, since the other ingredient was to be added by Fiedler, Mundt's second-in-command who happened to be Jewish, while Mundt, Leamas is told, is "quite the other thing." Hating Mundt, Fiedler should jump at the suggestion that he is a traitor. The film's first half focused on Leamas's pose as a disgruntled and discharged spy, taken to drink and fights with the local shopkeeper. Contacted by a series of middlemen, "cut-outs" in the spy's jargon, Leamas finally arrives at a Dutch seacoast village where he is interrogated by a calm, de-

Director Martin Ritt (left) with Richard Burton and Claire Bloom in front of London's Wormwood Scrubs Prison. *(The Spy Who Came in from the Cold)*

Karl-Dieter Mundt (left, Peter Van Eyck) confronts his quarry, Leamas (Richard Burton), in the appropriate setting for counterspy and spy. *(The Spy Who Came in from the Cold)*

tached professional agent. Their conversations end however, when news of Leamas's disappearance appears in a London newspaper—he must now head eastwards. Leamas protests, but then learns that neither the KGB nor their East German colleagues had leaked the news to the press. This is the first hint of a more complicated scheme than he has bar-

gained for, but Leamas lets himself be taken for further interrogation to East Germany, where he meets Fiedler.

In a series of well-crafted scenes between Fiedler and Leamas, the difference between the two professionals was highlighted. Their conversations and Mundt's unexpected arrival also lead to a fast-paced sequence of arrests,

In the East German countryside, Fiedler (right, Oskar Werner) could question Leamas (Richard Burton) without fear of being overheard. *(The Spy Who Came in from the Cold)*

releases and re-arrests, with Fiedler leveling the charge of treason at Mundt before a secret tribunal of the ruling Communist Party. Fiedler's circumstanial evidence is trumped by Mundt's witness, a young librarian and English Communist, Pam (Claire Bloom), who had been Leamas's lover during his pose as a disgruntled alcoholic. Pam supplies the needed evidence to indict Leamas as an agent planted on Fiedler to betray Mundt. At the hearing's

Comrade Fiedler (left, Oskar Werner) indicates to the arresting officer his suspect, Comrade Mundt (Peter Van Eyck), who has been interrogating Leamas (Richard Burton). *(The Spy Who Came in from the Cold)*

The secret tribunal begins with Fiedler's (left, Oskar Werner) examination of his witness, Leamas (Richard Burton), while Mundt (right, Peter Van Eyck) and his defense attorney (George Voskovec) look on. *(The Spy Who Came in from the Cold)*

Mundt's surprise witness, Nan Perry (Claire Bloom), takes the stand, while Alec Leamas (left rear, Richard Burton) begins to realize the danger he is in. *(The Spy Who Came in from the Cold)*

Comrade Fiedler (left, Oskar Werner) tries to explain Leamas' (right, Richard Burton) role in Mundt's actual treachery. *(The Spy Who Came in from the Cold)*

close it is Fiedler who is escorted out by uniformed guards, while Mundt stares icily at Leamas. Mundt, the audience and Pam later learn from Leamas, was indeed London's man and that the aim of this "dirty operation" was not to kill Mundt but rather to eliminate Fiedler, who had begun to suspect the truth.

The truth for the audience was that cold-blooded expediency was the sole criterion used by espionage chiefs on both sides of the Berlin Wall, which figures so prominently in Martin Ritt's film. Besides the near-betrayal of Leamas, a professional spy, the London spymasters had involved a total innocent, Pam, in their complex game of cross and double-cross. That Pam was an idealistic Communist who had fallen in love with Leamas only "made it easy" for the fatal mechanism to work more smoothly. The final irony was that Fiedler, condemned as a traitor by his own comrades, could see through the events that Mundt *had*

The innocent, Nan (Claire Bloom), takes a last look at East Berlin, while Leamas (Richard Burton) tries to pull her over the wall that will doom them both. *(The Spy Who Came in from the Cold)*

Diego (Yves Montand) examines a car being altered to smuggle political leaflets into Spain. *(La Guerre Est Finie)*

to be a double-agent, otherwise the lucky coincidence of Pam's arrival in East Germany and subsequent testimony could not have taken place. Throughout the film Fiedler was characterized as a curious combination of idealist and functionary who rebuked Leamas as the "lowest currency of the Cold War" and then asked what motivated Leamas to be a spy in the first place, what grand ideal. Fiedler was, of course, shocked at Leamas's total indifference to ideology. Mundt, on the other hand, was depicted as the brutal secret police officer familiar from wartime films, and the actor chosen for this part had indeed played Nazis in several Hollywood films. The audience's sympathy was divided between Leamas and Fiedler, particularly since the only times when the camera veered away from Burton was when Oskar Werner spoke.

The Spy Who Came in from the Cold was a landmark in film history; not only was it a seriously honest and grim portrayal of modern

A local drunkard (right, R. J. Chauffar) has just told Diego (left, Yves Montand) that he works for the police. *(La Guerre Est Finie)*

Nadine Sallanches (Genevieve Bujold) is comforted by the man she knows as Domingo (Yves Montand). *(La Guerre Est Finie)*

espionage, but it also avoided many of the hallowed traditions of the spy film. There were no car chases, fist fights, hidden bombs or extended shoot-outs, only the businesslike ma-

chine gun bursts at the Berlin Wall. There were no excessive scenes of torture nor long-winded explanations of the strategic importance of Leamas's assignment. Besides focusing on the moral ambiguity surrounding espionage work, the film also depicted an ostensible enemy in a sympathetic light. Despite these thematic innovations, *The Spy Who Came in from the Cold* was a conventional narrative. A 1967 European film merged its unconventional format to the story of one incident in a spy's life, *La Guerre Est Finie* (The War Is Over).

Directed by the New Wave filmmaker Alain Resnais, from a screenplay by an explicitly political writer, Jorge Semprun, *La Guerre Est Finie* focussed on the subjective, on the world and history as experienced by a middle-aged man who was not only a spy, but a revolutionary as well. In this film the audience had to piece together the memories and incidents reflected on the screen. The film's title referred ironically to the Spanish Civil War, still fought clandestinely by spies sent across the French border. One such agent was seen at the film's opening on his way back from Spain, while a voice-over and a series of rapid flash-forward scenes depicted the people in the spy's life. Resnais was constantly shifting between the objective and the subjective, between the real border crossing and the imagined or remembered episodes in the

Planning a mission in Barcelona, Diego (center, Yves Montand) studies a street map along with Roberto (left, Paul Crauchet) and Manolo (Jacques Rispal). *(La Guerre Est Finie)*

On his way to a meeting with Roberto (left, Paul Crauchet), Diego (Yves Montand) seems unaware of the wall poster calling for a demonstration against Franco. *(La Guerre Est Finie)*

the police phone call. When Diego meets to thank her for her help, they make love; there was an unabashed erotic quality to Diego's work as seen by Resnais. Women stare at Diego with frank, sexual interest, perhaps a concession to the tradition of Mata Hari and James Bond. At a second meeting with Nadine to return her father's passport, he sees policemen trailing her, and for an extended sequence the audience was treated to the sight of Diego following the policemen following Nadine. There were other traditional links to the familiar spy film: messages hidden in toothpaste tubes, the change of photos in legitimate passports and the alterations to a car's chassis to smuggle leaflets into Spain. Resnais' skill, however, lay in the balance between the dramatic and the mundane; each of the mechanical facets of espionage was balanced by the introduction of a new character, a new

protagonist's life (Yves Montand). Since much of the film was seen through his eyes and mind, there was a touch of confusion and unreality, just as he admitted that his whole identity was a falsehood fabricated to elude both the French and Spanish police. The audience didn't even learn his real name, Diego, until halfway through the film. Because of a series of arrests by the Spanish police, whether rumored or real remained unclear, Diego had returned prematurely to France to report this news to his superiors. He was also haunted by the thought, and the imagined scene, of a comrade's arrest. Diego's life as a professional revolutionary and spy, his attempt to warn his comrades, his meetings with the exile leaders and the details of espionage were all elements in this film, but the perspective and pacing were not at all traditional. The film was a slow, rhythmic march through the lives of the men and women whom Diego has met.

One of these women is a young student, Nadine (Genevieve Bujold), who is also involved in illegal political work in Spain. The falsified passport Diego has used belonged to Nadine's father, so that when Diego and his driver are stopped at the border for what he assumes is a routine border check, she answers

Marianne (Ingrid Thulin) comforts Diego (Yves Montand). *(La Guerre Est Finie)*

59

Nadine Sallanches (Genevieve Bujold) receives her father's passport, as well as a kiss, from Domingo (Yves Montand). *(La Guerre Est Finie)*

facet of Diego's personality or another piece of the puzzle linking the importance of events.

The politics in *La Guerre Est Finie* were both explicit and implicit. While going through the routine of changing identity papers after his mission, Diego jokes with his mirrored reflection about patience and irony being the virtues of a good Bolshevik. These qualities also describe his character, particularly during the long meetings at which Diego reports his findings and hears repeated the admonitions which his voice-over has anticipated. He is patiently ironic with Nadine, who represents a more radical and activist view toward the situation in Spain, a view which at times parallels his own opinion. There were visual clues to the political tone, as well: the Spanish Republican flag at the funeral of one of their number and a photograph of Fidel Castro in someone's apartment.

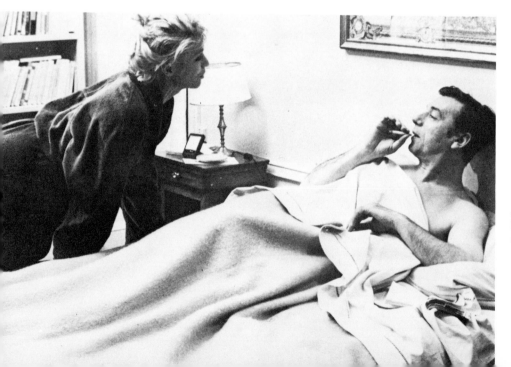

A spy (Yves Montand) and his lover, Marianne (Ingrid Thulin). *(La Guerre Est Finie)*

Carlos to his comrades in the clandestine organization; Domingo to the young student whose father's passport he has used; or Diego to his lover: the face of an aging secret agent (Yves Montand). *(La Guerre Est Finie)*

Will Geer in the role of oil tycoon
Ferguson. *(Executive Action)*

There was also the tone of the characters' lives as they vacillated between French and Spanish in their conversations, an aural indication of a cause almost lost. Political reality and illusion frequently clashed in this failure of ideological nerve. Diego had assumed that the border check was a routine procedure and did not mention it to his comrades, but Nadine realized that it was Diego who had inadvertently put the police on her trail. At the film's climax, Diego returns to Spain to carry out another mission.

Diego's screen antecedent was Kurt Muller: both were exiles facing death by returning to their own country; both symbolize a generation hardened by violent political defeats and both draw strength from the women in their lives. At the close of the film, Diego's mistress, Marianne (Ingrid Thulin), accepts the responsibility to fly to Spain to warn Diego of an expected trap, just as he had hoped to warn his contact. The film has come full cycle, as the screen flash-forwards to Marianne's vision of the meeting with Diego. The uncertainty of her mission, like the aging, worried faces of Diego's comrades, gave the film its tragic tone. This was reinforced by slow tracking shots and melancholy music, so that *La Guerre Est Finie* was a requiem for the pensive radicals whose failures and tragedies dotted so

Former CIA agent Farrington (right, Burt Lancaster) shows schemer Foster (left, Robert Ryan) a photo of Lee Harvey Oswald. *(Executive Action)*

much of modern European history. Fearful of apprehension by their enemies, Resnais and Semprun's characters suffered the worse dread, that their aims and methods were totally illusory.

This particularly leftist malaise, however, was only a part of the general disillusionment with political beliefs. The Cold War's fervent anti-Communism could not withstand the fact of stability in Eastern Europe and China, any more than the Marxist idealist could accept the details of actual Communist Party rule. The real sinews of power lay in massive mechanized armies, bomber fleets and nuclear-tipped missiles, not in popular insurrection. Mundt's victory in *The Spy Who Came in from the Cold* was symbolic of this period: not only was a spy a conscious adversary, he was also a professional technician for whom political choices differed little from choice of weapons. It was not until the late 1960's that a second war in Indochina revived radical political movements among large and youthful populations in North America and Europe. The threat or hope for social revolution, depend-

ing upon which side of the barricade you saw yourself, seemed to lurk below the surface of the youths' rebellion and the waves of protest that followed in the wake of every bombing mission over Southeast Asia. The illusion of revolt haunted both cinema screens and police department budgets, and it was not long before U.S. government policies became the topic of spy and thriller films.

The Spy Who Came in from the Cold showed filmmakers that audiences would accept fictional treatments of real intrigues. In *Z* Constantine Costa-Gavras grafted the story of the military take-over in Greece onto a carefully unfolded murder-mystery, and Gillo Pontecorvo gave a guerilla movement lasting cinematic interpretation in *The Battle of Algiers.* Hollywood was not slow to recognize topics that could draw people to the box office. While many mediocre films were released dealing with young people and "life-style" issues, some directors and script writers did try to tackle relatively controversial issues. John F. Kennedy's assassination was ready-made for a spy film; there was a complex net of circumstances

Robert Ryan as the right-wing conspirator Foster. (*Executive Action*)

surrounding the actual event and a whole series of rumors that had not been stilled by an official investigation, as well as the drama of an attractive young president shot in front of his wife during a ceremonial motorcade. If only a portion of the rumored conspiracies did exist, the ramifications were both ominous and widespread. The distrust of government and the idealistic hope that something could be done to effect change united with the popular attachment to spies and melodrama in *Executive Action*.

Written by another veteran of the Hollywood blacklist, Dalton Trumbo, *Executive Action* used a variety of techniques: newsreels, simulated events and voice-overs, to weave a

Burt Lancaster as the former CIA agent Farrington. (*Executive Action*)

The right-wing Foster (left, Robert Ryan) and his hired CIA expert, Farrington (Burt Lancaster). *(Executive Action)*

conspiracy by multibillionaires and former government officials to murder the nation's leader. Although there were intimations in the film of involvement by CIA and White House personnel in the plot, this 1973 film's major point was that Lee Harvey Oswald was not the lone assassin. Underlining this idea was an inter-title and voice-over quotation from Kennedy's successor, Lyndon Johnson, to this effect. The credits then rolled over a series of shots of oil wells, derricks and prairie that establish the plot's funding by a Texan oil-tycoon, Ferguson (Will Geer), under the influence and tutelage of right-winger Foster (Robert Ryan).

Amid the luxuries of teak- and walnut-panelled rooms furnished with antiques, the two men repeat their reasons for killing Kennedy: the threat to remove troops from Vietnam, a rumored detente with the Soviets and what they see as the President's bid to lead the Civil Rights movement. Though realistically questionable motives, considering the gravity of the Cuban missile crisis, they were representative of the ideological posture of right-wing prejudices, southwest regionalism and petrochemical wealth. Neither Foster nor Ferguson are in government nor in a position to know Kennedy's daily movements, so they have to hire someone who is. A former CIA agent, Farrington (Burt Lancaster), joins the conspiracy as a consultant with contacts and friends in high government positions. A professional who does not agree totally with his employers, yet who skillfully carries out their orders, Farrington confides, in one scene, that this particular assignment will be his last. Foster makes sure it is.

Neither a detailed legal brief nor a documentary, *Executive Action* allowed for, indeed, created wide areas of ambiguity and doubt. Its allegorical tone could be judged from the mere choice of the characters' names, Ferguson, Foster and Farrington with the near ring of Dickensian whimsy. Coming ten years, nearly to the day, after the actual assassination, *Executive Action* incorporated many of the theories about the incident. A "second Oswald" was hired by the plotters to make himself conspicuous around Dallas, while three professional riflemen practiced their marks-

manship in the foothills of the Rockies with moving targets in the shape of an auto's silhouette. The real Oswald, his name the product of a computer search for a likely fall-guy, was depicted as something of an enigma with unexplained ties to the CIA and U.S. Navy Intelligence. More important in the film were the hints of cooperation from important allies in government: the disruption of phone communications within the capital on the day of the murder; the re-routing of the motorcade and the disappearance of the Cabinet's code book from their plane were events that did actually occur, not the figments of Trumbo's imagination. That only people close to the presidential staff could have arranged these accidents was a conclusion left to the audience. Director David Miller had not forgotten that he was dealing with relatively "hot" material, despite its fictional format.

The object of all this planning was, of course, Kennedy, who appeared in carefully

edited newsreel footage as the idealized popular leader in his prime. The President was shown greeting civil rights leaders, meeting his children and at various political rallies in the film's sympathetic portrait. Almost in conscious parody of the routine spy film, Foster lamented the inefficiency with which the Secret Service protected their intended victim. Cutting from actual newsreel scenes to simulated details, Miller's film climaxed with the assassination.

More unexpected and dramatic, however —after all, everyone knew that a successful assassination had been completed—was the screenful of eighteen faces. These eighteen people, some of whom still can be seen smiling at their photographer, were witnesses to the murder and had died within the intervening ten years. Given their ages and relative states of health, the film commented, such a series of deaths should have a chance of one in a trillion. As a cinematic hint of a real menace, as proof of some vast undiscovered conspiracy, these faces hinted more strongly than the bulk

of the film.

Death and deceit were not new to the spy film; they had been essential ingredients since the twenties. Politics did give substance and tone to a protagonist's moves; few people could condemn Kurt Muller in *Watch on the Rhine,* just as presumably even fewer could countenance John Jefferson's betrayal of mother and country in *My Son John.* It took nearly a decade for audiences to see the wry humor which had Roger Thornhill clamber around the faces carved into Mount Rushmore in his escape from Soviet spies and another five years before movie goers could accept the murderous double-cross in *The Spy Who Came in from the Cold.* Ideology and political belief no longer were clues to morality in the serious spy film; indeed politics and morality had become the worst of enemies. If audiences began to question the spy's motives, to weigh rights and wrongs, so did the celluloid agents. Below the surface of many films rested the rich soil of means and ends, and a few films began to tackle the problem of loyalty.

One of the two teams of gunmen hired by Ferguson. *(Executive Action)*

3

The Problem of Loyalty

Bridie Quilty (Deborah Kerr), threatened by the traditional figure of the spy in this publicity photo for *The Adventuress*.

The Measures Taken
The Adventuress
Decision Before Dawn
The Deadly Affair
Scorpio
State of Siege
Three Days of the Condor

"What horror would you not commit to put an end to horror?" asked the German playwright Bertolt Brecht in *The Measures Taken* (*Die Massnahme*), a short didactic piece written shortly before he fled Hitler. That was the question posed to the spy who realized that she or he might have to commit heinous crimes justifiable only by the victory of one nation or cause over another. Once that goal became questionable, then an entire life's work, and in the case of the espionage agent, life itself, was in danger. Since indirect strategems and ambiguity marked the spy's work, the test of ends-justifying-means could not be easily applied. And when a spy did realize that the nation or cause was not worth the crimes he was asked to perform, there were few alternatives. This problem of loyalty had a ready appeal to an audience; it posed a difficult choice for a protagonist already in a hazardous profession; it let the viewers weigh the moral debits and credits; and it could twist an audience's emotions by confronting mutually exclusive values, such as morality and expediency. This theme also allowed the exposure

of a spy system's abuses, since double-dealing and treachery are inevitable by-products of a spy's work. Loyalty could also be doubly dramatic, on both the personal and abstract levels; loyalty to an ideal may be linked to the betrayal of a friend. A wife's imagined infidelity could have a complementing dose of treason, while the price of loyalty alone could be inhumanly high. Whether a nation's people or a government's demands, the spy film could treat the whole concept of loyalty. Although serious detective and cowboy films occasionally raised similar issues, the spy film could draw the most explicit lessons for its audience. Hot wars, as well as cold ones, became appropriate backdrops for clandestine operators, while controversial portrayals of the CIA found ready support in newspaper accounts and Congressional hearings.

In a postwar film directed and written by Frank Launder, a semi-comic approach was applied to the problem of treachery and espionage. His first directorial effort, Launder's *The Adventuress* (sometimes billed as *I See a Dark Stranger*) used a gentle irony that occa-

Trevor Howard in a publicity still from 1946, between *Brief Encounter* and *The Adventuress*.

sionally lapsed into the absurd. Set in wartime Great Britain, this 1947 film concerned a young Irish woman's traditional dislike of the English that led her to assist German spies. Bridie Quilty (Deborah Kerr) was something of a traditional figure, the romantic, moody Irish woman with more spirit than apparent sense. Raised on stories and legends about the days of the Irish Republican Army's Great Rebellion in 1916, Bridie nurses both a grudge against the English dating from Oliver Cromwell, and a desire to become a legendary IRA heroine. In 1944, at the age of 21, Bridie leaves her home village of Balleygary for Dublin, to join the IRA. Her encounter with a famed rebel officer, now a respected art museum curator, does not assuage her fury. Un-

daunted she sails to England where she soon finds suitable targets for her rage. In a small English village where she works in the local inn, the town square's statue of Cromwell is defaced by paint, but Bridie's private war is not fought merely by symbolic attack. She has been contacted by a German agent named Miller (Raymond Huntley).

A good part of the film's charm lay in the contrast between Bridie and Miller. He is the cool, detached professional while Bridie is tempestuous, enraged and a thorough-going amateur. Miller had noticed her on the packet boat from Ireland feverishly studying a German grammar book, although he looked and acted like an average middle-class, English businessman, down to the casual reading of

Miller (Raymond Huntley), as first seen by Bridie (Deborah Kerr), is the picture of the typical Englishman. *(The Adventuress)*

Baynes (Trevor Howard), who has recently arrived at the village inn. Miller rightly suspects that Baynes is a counterspy. Although helping a German agent, Bridie has retained her good, Irish Catholic morals and is shocked by Miller's suggestion that she feign a romantic interest in Baynes to lure him away from the town for several valuable hours. This obvious parody of the traditional Mata Hari role was intensified by both Bridie's apprehensive interior monologue and Launder's spoken dialogue. When told that Baynes might be an intelligence officer, she tells Miller that the young lieutenant didn't seem all that intelligent to her, and when she reproaches Baynes for being a "fast worker" in asking for a date,

The Economist. (This characterization was helped immeasurably by type-casting, since Huntley has traditionally played undersecretaries, assistant bank managers and civil servants, with wonderful regularity.)

Bridie's major function is to supply Miller with the information she gleans from soldiers stationed at a military prison near the village. One of Miller's spies is held there, an important agent with valuable information whom Miller must free. His plan soon becomes endangered when Miller notices a young officer,

German spy Oscar Pryce (David Ward) silhouetted against wall of peculiar town, in pre-credit opening sequence. *(The Adventuress)*

73

Bridie Quilty (Deborah Kerr) receives her instructions from Miller (Raymond Huntley). *(The Adventuress)*

he explains by telling her that he had been working with the American troops.

The script's humor even extended to what has usually been a most traditionally melodramatic sequence—a dying Miller giving Bridie further instructions. Sitting in an armchair with his tie askew, as if he had had a hard day's work, it is only the music and lighting which give him a fatal appearance. When Bridie frantically pleads with him to see a doctor, he coolly explains that he needs an operation, not a doctor, since there's a bullet inside him. Incredulous, she asks how he could possibly know, and Miller sarcastically replies, "Because it didn't come out." Even Miller's ostensible loyalty to the Third Reich is questionable, since he tells her to tell a certain Hungarian countess that he died for Germany, as it

Bridie Quilty (Deborah Kerr) has more on her mind than the company of the infatuated Lieutenant Baynes (Trevor Howard). *(The Adventuress)*

Miller (Raymond Huntley) knows something of which Lieutenant David Baynes (right, Trevor Howard) has not an inkling. *(The Adventuress)*

The German spy Oscar Pryce (David Ward), walking the streets of a peculiar town in the pre-credit opening sequence. *(The Adventuress)*

should amuse her. Besides having to dispose of his body, which Bridie does by using her invalid employer's wheelchair, she has to convey an important message about a hidden notebook to a contact on a train.

On her own, Bridie must face all the traditional problems of the spy as reflected in Launder's satirical screenplay. She immediately gets flustered on the train when one of her fellow passengers, a naval officer, opens the window, depriving her of the predetermined recognition phrase. Finally able to ask for the window to be opened again, there is no response from any of the passengers as Bridie

German agent (Katie Johnson) escorted from train by two plainclothesmen. *(The Adventuress)*

Pryce (center, David Ward) is handed over to another spy, Hawkins (left, Michael Howard), by unsuspecting army sergeant. *(The Adventuress)*

Bridie (second from right, Deborah Kerr) must determine which of her fellow passengers is a contact, or "cut-out." *(The Adventuress)*

and the camera search each face for a clue. Low-angle shots, dim lighting and her frantic interior monologue all aid the paranoid vision of the train compartment. When a team of policemen enters the compartment to make an arrest, she is about to stand up in response to their imperious "come-along-with-us-please." Filmed at an angle so as to confuse the exact object of their demand, the scene reveals that the little old lady sitting next to her is her fellow spy. Bridie must now go to the Isle of Man to fetch the secret notebook.

It is while in the picturesque little town on the Channel Island that Bridie has to confront

Goodhusband (right, Garry Marsh) asserts impossibility of capturing anyone from the meager description, while Spanswick (left, Tom Macaulay) looks doubtful. (The Adventuress)

Captain Goodhusband (Garry Marsh) receives phone call about description of Bridie, while Lieutenant Spanswick (Tom Macaulay) begins to worry and a corporal prepares to take a memo. (The Adventuress)

Bridie (Deborah Kerr) checks into local hotel, fearful of capture, after Miller's death. (The Adventuress)

Having found the notebook secreted by Pryce, Bridie (Deborah Kerr) realizes that it contains information about the invasion of Europe. *(The Adventuress)*

her feelings of loyalty and treachery. She has discovered the notebook, and a casual reading of its listing of French names and mysterious numbers acts as a revelation. The coded references refer to the invasion, she thinks aloud to herself, and more importantly to British lives and *Irish* lives, while the screen is filled with staged scenes of German military preparations and English dead. She returns to her hotel room and prepares to burn the book, when Lieutenant Baynes appears. Not only has

Baynes been on her trail, but she has also been spotted by a German agent. Despite Baynes' love for her and her intention to become a retired spy, Bridie Quilty must now avoid capture by the British military, now alert to her importance, and abduction by German agents. Bridie and Baynes do get caught, however, by spies who, like Miller, are typically English figures, although significantly a degree or two lower in the social order.

The two spies try to enter Ireland by becoming part of a horse-drawn funeral procession that turns out to be, just within yards of the border, a smuggling expedition complete to a coffin full of alarm clocks. In the hilarious melee, Bridie and Baynes escape to a pub they think is in Ireland. When they realize they are in Northern Ireland, Baynes heads with Bridie for the border so as to be able to hand her over to the Irish authorities for violation of neutrality rather than to the English as a spy. This madcap romance within a spy film format ends as it began, in a country inn where the newly wed Baynes couple have arrived for a honeymoon; then she looks out the window and stalks out, baggage in hand. She is last

For Goodhusband (center, Garry Marsh), a routine check on identity papers is an excuse to flirt with Bridie (Deborah Kerr), who fears the worst, and a matter of efficient surveillance for Spanswick (left, Tom Macaulay). *(The Adventuress)*

seen by a bewildered husband and an amused audience within sight of the inn's signboard flapping in the wind, The Cromwell Arms.

The Adventuress was a satirical stew of many spy film elements: there was the suspense of a young woman becoming a part of a German spy circuit and her effort to escape; her romance with her ostensible opponent

While dancing with Bridie (Deborah Kerr), Captain Goodhusband (Garry Marsh) sees (and is seen by) his wife. *(The Adventuress)*

Finally able to play the heroine, Bridie Quilty (Deborah Kerr) appears more resolute than Baynes (right, Trevor Howard) when confronting the enemy agent (Norman Shelley). *(The Adventuress)*

and the general problem of Irish–English hatreds. In accordance with Launder's style these themes were handled with a gentle, if almost absurd, irony. The caricatured English behavior of the bumbling army commander on the Isle of Man and of the spies themselves was complemented by the caricatured heroine. Obsessed with delusions of IRA glory, Bridie was both protagonist and the object of English condescension. Romantic, far-fetched, Bridie was the temperamental colleen who emerged unscathed from encounters with Nazi agents, British army officers and romantic counterspies. Her rebelliousness was even carried through to the film's close, in her hatred of anything to do with Cromwell. Her disloyalty was cast as a parody of Irish attitudes as much as a satire of the traditional spy film format. Miller's death, the confrontation on the train, and the actual kidnapping were comic, with an emphasis on human frailty and

eccentricities rather than on intrigue or violence. The only serious note was Bridie's reflection on the real meaning of the information she had so diligently retrieved. A far grimmer vision of the wartime conflict of loyalties came from Hollywood in the 1952 film *Decision Before Dawn*.

While Launder had chosen a born romantic torn between her instinct for rebellion and her common sense, Anatole Litvak's film focused on a German prisoner-of-war, a Luftwaffe medic (Oskar Werner), who volunteers to be a spy for the Americans after witnessing the murder of a fellow POW by fanatically loyal Nazis. Screened by American intelligence officer (Richard Basehart and Gary Merrill) who are suspicious of the motives of the Germans who come to them, the medic, code named Happy, is sent to a special school where his native idealism and charm are seen in encounters with other volunteers and their

The funeral cortege turns out to be a procession of smugglers, much to the shame of the chief mourner (right, Harry Hutchinson). *(The Adventuress)*

instructors. Some of the volunteers are motivated by both the mundane need for security in postwar Germany and lingering resentment against the Nazis. One volunteer, code named Tiger (Hans Christian Blech), is chosen just because he has such obviously selfish reasons for helping the Americans. Sent behind the crumbling German lines, Happy and Tiger must determine the exact whereabouts of a specific Panzer division threatening the Allied advance.

During his journey through the battered cities of his homeland, Happy meets many typical Germans; some reinforce while others endanger his resolve to help his American superiors. His loyalty to a relatively new cause comes smack up against the familiarity of his own people.

Litvak's film was a graphic depiction of the torn fabric left of the Third Reich: the tawdry, sad wantonness of the canteen–hostel where women amuse the transient population of soldiers and railway men; the constant search by military police and SS units for the

Still the Irish rebel, the newly married Mrs. David Baynes (Deborah Kerr) glares up at the name of the hotel in which she refuses to stay. (*The Adventuress*)

A cynical Colonel Devlin (Garry Merrill) examines the paybook of the Luftwaffe medic to be code-named Happy (left, Oskar Werner). *(Decision Before Dawn)*

During his training Happy (Oskar Werner) meets Monique (Dominique Blanchar). *(Decision Before Dawn)*

traitors and defeatists whose bodies, adorned with placards, dangle from the occasional lamp post, and the mounds of rubble that serve as the backdrop to the scenes caught by Franz Planer's camera. The people are also leftovers of a destroyed empire: some, like the SS courier Scholtz (Wilfried Seyfert), boast drunkenly of the dozen years that the world will never forget, while others, like the canteen girl Hilde (Hildegarde Neff), are burnt-out ciphers. Between these personal encounters, Happy evades the SS and Gestapo men who comb the huge masses of disorganized soldiery fleeing across the Rhine. Weekly lists are issued to the security police with the names and identity numbers of suspected

During coffee break, producer-director Anatole Litvak chats with Oskar Werner and Dominique Blanchar. *(Decision Before Dawn)*

spies, and Happy's eyes are inevitably drawn to these sheets. Constant surveillance and the ever-present fear of arrest mark the film's tone, as it depicts the dogged persistence with which the Nazi secret police protect a defeated regime from its internal enemies. Happy is curiously the mirror reversal of that devotion, since he too strains every nerve to help his former enemies.

That mirror image receives its proper framework; Happy is requisitioned and drafted into a scratch unit by a roving band of junior officers and sergeants. Happy has been assigned as personal medic to the commander of the same Panzer division he had been ordered to locate. During the night that commander is saved from a heart attack by Happy's prompt and competent treatment. In

Another German volunteer (seated, center, Hans Christian Blech) gets appraised by Colonel Devlin (left, Gary Merrill) and Lieutenant Rennick (right, Richard Basehart). *(Decision Before Dawn)*

Hilde (Hildegarde Neff) is both amused and surprised by Happy's (Oskar Werner) politeness. *(Decision Before Dawn)*

Happy (Oskar Werner) accidentally meets an old family friend, Fraulein Schneider (Helene Thimig). *(Decision Before Dawn)*

return the Herr Oberstgeneral grants Happy a favor, but not the one which the young idealist requests, that a young soldier sentenced to be executed be spared. The following morning, with a travel pass authorized by the division commander, Happy leaves with the exact coordinates of the unit. His trip back to the Allied lines, however, is not as easy. In the course of an Allied strafing he learns that his name and identity number have been included on the latest Gestapo list of suspects. Happy must make contact with Tiger, if he wants to get his news to the Americans.

Tiger, whose loyalty to his new bosses was based on expediency, has been waiting for the war to pass over him and end, rather than endanger his life by spying. Neither a Nazi villain nor an anti-Nazi hero, Tiger wishes to remain neutral. That neutrality disappears when Happy arrives with the Gestapo and mil-

Fraulein Schneider (Helene Thimig) hears the false name Happy (center, Oskar Werner) has given the traffic control officer. *(Decision Before Dawn)*

The division commander, *Oberst* Von Ecker (O. E. Hasse), tells Happy (Oskar Werner) his duties as Von Ecker's personal medical orderly. *(Decision Before Dawn)*

itary police a few steps behind. If only to save his own skin, Tiger has to help get Happy across the American lines. The film's irony is that Happy dies in that attempt while Tiger survives and manages to bring the American officers their desired information. That Tiger had done relatively little to merit their praise and that Happy's death was greeted with a casual remark about his being "just another Kraut," showed the near futility of Happy's idealistic treachery.

For American or British audiences it was fairly easy to identify with Happy against the brutalities of his Nazi countrymen. As played by Werner, Happy was the ideal, good German—polite, intelligent and full of remorse over what his nation had done. The audience already knows that he acts out of the purest motives, so that the two U.S. Army officers appear overly cynical. Even one of the espionage school instructors finds herself drawn to Happy, although she brusquely tells him that her lover has been shot by Germans. For both filmmakers and audience it was far easier to

Happy (right, Oskar Werner) finds himself recruited into the *Panzerdivision* he had been ordered to locate. *(Decision Before Dawn)*

85

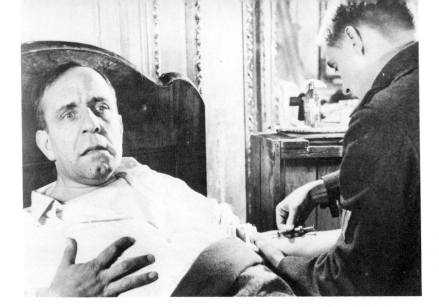

Happy (right, Oskar Werner) manages to save the colonel's (O. E. Hasse) life. *(Decision Before Dawn)*

examine, accept and watch the disloyalty of an idealistic German towards a regime guilty of war crimes than to show the ideals which motivated an American or Englishman to become a spy for the Soviet Union.

In the Cold War spy films it was typical to depict these characters as the pliable victims of ruthless cynics or as psychologically unstable personalities as in *The Iron Curtain* and *My Son John*. The success of *The Spy Who Came in from the Cold* was prepared by several years of publicity afforded real espionage activity that had gone sour. The embarrassment surrounding

the U-2 affair, when an American reconnaissance aircraft was shot down over Soviet territory, not only ended a summit meeting scheduled between Eisenhower and Khruschev in Paris, but also brought the CIA to the attention of the newspaper reader. A year later when Cuban exiles funded and trained by the CIA attempted the abortive invasion of Cuba at the Bay of Pigs, national attention and concern grew over the mysterious power of the CIA to risk American lives and the threat of war in its clandestine operations. The strange alliances and complex intrigues extended into

Having dumped his incriminating identification papers, Happy (right, Oskar Werner) is the natural target of the SS officer's suspicions. *(Decision Before Dawn)*

...ing killed a Gestapo agent, Happy (Oskar Werner) discov-...his name on the weekly list of suspects. *(Decision Before* ...*n)*

Tiger (right, Hans Christian Blech) is about to douse the match that Happy (Oskar Werner) has innocently struck while searching for Tiger. *(Decision Before Dawn)*

Europe as well. In 1963 the West Germans discovered that their own espionage department had been infiltrated by Soviet agents for over ten years. In a story still clouded by official secrets, Reinhard Gehlen, the Wehrmacht's former expert on the Red Army, had built up his own private spy organization with the CIA's help. The American spy masters had the dubious honor of lavishly funding the employment of former SS and Gestapo officers who had been stationed during the war in occupied Russia, while their Soviet counterparts were busily sending their own operatives to the Gehlen organization. Nazi or Communist, American or Russian, CIA or KGB—it seemed to differ little to the professional spies whose faces began to appear with greater frequency in the world's press.

The personal dimension to the controversy and intrigue over rival ideologies and shifting professional allegiances were caught in another of Le Carré's filmed novels, *The Deadly Affair.* In this 1966 film the problem of loyalty was played against the domestic drama of marital infidelity. Produced and directed by Sidney Lumet from a screenplay by Paul

Caught attempting to swim over to the American lines, Happy (Oskar Werner) is led away to be shot. *(Decision Before Dawn)*

Inspector Mendel (Harry Andrews) dozes among his pets, with notes on the Fennan case in his lap. *(The Deadly Affair)*

Inspector Mendel (Harry Andrews) coaxes some information from Virgin (Lynn Redgrave), the student actress. *(The Deadly Affair)*

Dehn, the film opened with the routine investigation of a British Foreign Office staff member who had been anonymously accused of treason. Security checks and loyalty tests were not new in the 1960's; in America state employees routinely signed loyalty oaths and in England, where an Official Secrets Acts existed, high-level defections and information leaks had made the headlines. So it was not unusual that an experienced secret service agent, Charles Dobbs (James Mason), was assigned the task of conducting the security investigation in *The Deadly Affair*. During a lunch time conversation in Hyde Park with Dobbs, the suspect official, Fennan (Robert Flemyng), admits flirting with Communism

Elsa Fennan (Simone Signoret) meets her control, Dieter Frey (Maximilian Schell), in the trap set for them by Dobbs. *(The Deadly Affair)*

back in Oxford during the 1930's but voices his current disillusionment with both the Soviet Union and Communist Party. Convinced that Fennan is not a security risk and could be considered for promotion, Dobbs is bewildered by the man's later suicide and a note confessing treachery. Dobbs' doubts about his perception of Fennan's innocence and his ability as an intelligence officer are linked to his marital problems. He is plagued by the uncertainty of his wife's faithfulness and assumes that she has been engaged in a number of love affairs. Mirroring his own domestic drama, the Fennan case involves the man's widow, Elsa (Simone Signoret), a survivor of a Nazi death camp who might be a witness to her husband's guilt or innocence. Not only does Dobbs have to resign from the Secret Service to pursue a private investigation, but he also has to face a real break with his wife whose

Charles Dobbs (left, James Mason) and Bill Appleby (Kenneth Haigh) peer at the person who will fall into their trap for the enemy control. *(The Deadly Affair)*

lover happens to be Dobbs' wartime friend, Dieter Frey (Maximilian Schell).

Frey turns out to be the answer to both the espionage and domestic dilemma. Not only is Frey revealed as his wife's lover; he is also shown to be Elsa Fennan's "control," the spy who operated her work. Fearing betrayal at the hands of Elsa, who has merely been tricked by a wartime postal card ploy developed by Dobbs and Frey, Frey kills her, just as he had killed her husband and several others in his unsuccessful efforts to evade Dobbs.

Dehn's screenplay did not call for simple denunciations of Communist traitors and murder. Dobbs had seen one man, upset over his wife's treachery, nearly implicate himself out of love for her, while Dobbs himself has

had to kill a man he once respected and liked. Frustrated over the pointless deaths connected with the Fennan case, as well as the petty annoyances posed by his superior, Dobbs resigns from the espionage game. It was this tension between personal feelings and official duties that served as the film's real focus, since there was not one mention of any specific secret—the Foreign Office was just a "MacGuffin" to begin the drama between Dobbs and Frey. As an effective and intelligent spy, Dobbs was contrasted with his role as a passive and insecure husband, while Dobbs' ally, a retired police inspector, Mendel (Harry Andrews), was seen as both a tough cop and an aging civil servant napping amid his collection of exotic pets. In all the lives portrayed

Unarmed, Dobbs (back to camera, James Mason) must face his former wartime friend Frey (Maximilian Schell), who has revealed himself as the murderous enemy agent Dobbs has sought. *(The Deadly Affair)*

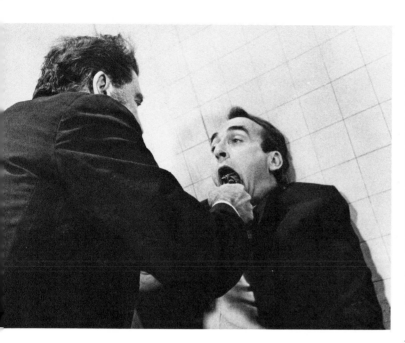

Cross (Burt Lancaster) has captured the CIA agent assigned to tail him. *(Scorpio)*

Cross (right, Burt Lancaster) gives Jean "Scorpio" Laurier (Alain Delon) a few words of advice upon their arrival at Dulles International Airport. *(Scorpio)*

espionage was a totally destructive element: five people, as well as Frey, die and at the film's conclusion a battered but wiser Dobbs is seen sipping a martini, on his way to Switzerland to meet his wife and the life of a retired spy.

Retirement, however, was not always possible for a spy, particularly an agent caught in the no-man's-land between the two superpowers. Cross (Burt Lancaster) was such a spy

in the 1972 Anglo-American production *Scorpio*. Released at a time when disclosures about CIA and FBI abuses were receiving wider acceptance, *Scorpio* might have become a controversial success, but was forestalled by Costa-Gavras' more factual *State of Siege*. A peculiarly melodramatic and grim spy film, *Scorpio* had two rival protagonists: Cross, an experienced CIA agent being hunted by his former colleagues, and a former French paratroop officer, Jean Laurier (Alain Delon), now a "CIA contract button man," a professional assassin, code-named Scorpio. Irked by the

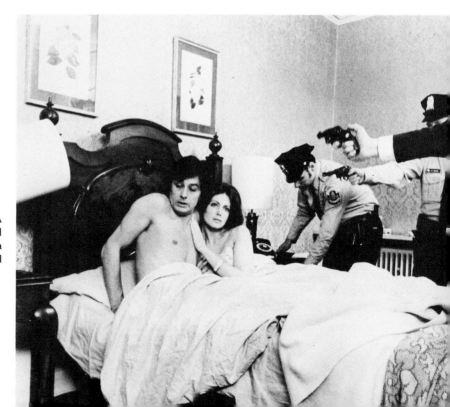

Caught by the local police in a CIA frame-up, Laurier (Alain Delon) will have no choice but to hunt Cross in a path that leads to his lover, Susan (Gail Hunnicut). *(Scorpio)*

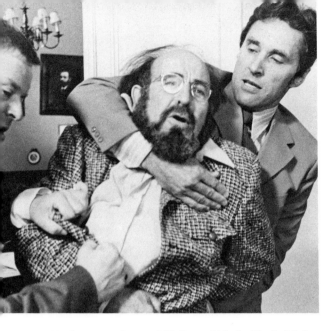

CIA hirelings Dor (George Mikell), and Novin (Frederick Jaeger) work over Cross's friend Lang (Shmul Rodensky). *(Scorpio)*

Cross (right, Burt Lancaster) discusses his escape from the country with Washington, D.C., friend Pick (Melvin Stewart). *(Scorpio)*

Frenchman's independence, the CIA chief McLeod (John Colicos) has had heroin planted in his bedroom to make the hired killer more pliable. Threatened with a drug arrest, Scorpio has no choice but to accept the assignment to kill Cross, although McLeod sugars the pill with promises of a fat bonus and Cross' job as the CIA's man in the Near East. Although told that Cross has been a double-agent working for the "opposition," Scorpio remains doubtful. In the meantime, by a series of clever tricks and tactics, Cross has not only managed to evade the CIA men follow-

ing him, but has arrived in the favorite city for cinematic intrigue and celluloid spies, Vienna.

The bulk of the film's action and some of its best sequences take place in the former imperial capital where the mystery surrounding Cross deepens. In a nighttime rendezvous on a deserted street, Cross is met by a Viennese sanitation worker who is whistling, perhaps as a signal or out of habit, the "Internationale."

CIA Chief McLeod (John Colicos) considers Laurier's (right, Alain Delon) demands for both money and a staff position in the agency. *(Scorpio)*

93

KGB man Zharkov (Paul Scofield) takes aim at the CIA man in the back seat. *(Scorpio)*

The husky-voiced Cross says, "It's been a long time since Spain," to which the man responds, "The best died there," and gives Cross directions to meet two more "cut-outs." This kind of political reference occurred frequently in the film's dialogue as part of the sympathetic characterization of Cross as envisioned by script writer David Rintels. In a sequence that was easily the equal of some of the best spy films, Cross and his Soviet counterpart, Serge Zharkov (Paul Scofield), laughingly discuss their mutual scorn for their bosses and the identical young men who staff both the CIA and KGB. While Cross good-naturedly accepts Zharkov's evaluation of themselves as a pair of premature anti-fascists, he can not understand Zharkov's professed belief in Communism after years spent in a Stalinist labor

Cross (Burt Lancaster) discovers Lang's body. *(Scorpio)*

camp and the recent invasion of Czechoslovakia. In a later scene when Zharkov tries to get help from his superiors and is refused, the embassy official is given a dose of Zharkov's irony when told of his resemblance to another man "who didn't leave his name, but was trying to build socialism in one country out of the bones from a charnel house"—as strong an indictment of Stalin's Russia as any Cold War film, but more intelligent and more skillfully presented.

Laurier, code-named Scorpio (Alain Delon), searches through Susan's things in a quest for clues. *(Scorpio)*

Scorpio's major element was the state of tension in which the audience was held; until the final quarter-hour viewers could not be certain if Cross was indeed a double-agent or a CIA maverick, an eccentric hated by the human automatons represented by McLeod. The CIA chief appeared more ruthless than

Behind the paper bag is the gun with which Cross (Burt Lancaster) will kill McLeod. *(Scorpio)*

95

Having shot down his lover, Susan, "Scorpio (Alain Delon) waits to hear Cross's confession of disloyalty before killing him, too. *(Scorpio)*

Laurier (Alain Delon) guns down Cross (Burt Lancaster). The evidence that sealed his fate lies on the floor before him. *(Scorpio)*

any other character; he was willing to frame Scorpio on a false charge, to endanger his own agents needlessly and even to have Cross's wife murdered in a bungled burglary attempt. There was even a hint of Nazi hirelings, since one of Cross's wartime friends, Max (Shmul Rodensky), was killed during an interrogation conducted by a local Viennese thug who had laughed slyly at the mention of Max's imprisonment in a concentration camp.

The problem of Cross's guilt or innocence centered on Scorpio, who knew enough to distrust McLeod yet was honor bound to fulfill his assignment. In a nighttime scene shot in a huge enclosed botanical garden, Scorpio meets Cross and their dialogue is a clever mix-

bullet-filled action scenes that owed more to James Bond than to Alfred Hitchcock. There was also a schizophrenic division in the film between the dialogue and the shoot-outs. At times the tricks by which one spy eluded the other were indeed clever, just the thing an average person could do if had thought about it, while at other times they strained credulity, for instance Cross's impersonation of a Black clergyman.

Cross almost escapes the CIA and Scorpio until the bungled burglary and his wife's death draw him back to Washington to kill McLeod. That successful assassination results in a leadership change and the near resignation of Scorpio, who is sickened by what he sees as the CIA's penchant for gratuitous murder and paranoid delusion. Both Scorpio and

Turner (Robert Redford) watches his colleague-lover, Janice (Tina Chen), correct his calligraphy. *(Three Days of the Condor)*

ture of plot development and characterization. To the Frenchman's direct question whether he is a traitor or not, Cross tells Scorpio that he reminds him of a little girl in her white Communion dress looking for God, but that since Scorpio has the soul of a killer his need is even greater. Cross denies being a double-agent and just as a trio of CIA men come crashing into the garden tells Scorpio that McLeod wanted him killed as well. The sequence ends with automatic slugs resounding among the ferns and flowers.

This sequence also displayed one of the film's worst features, the awkward transitions from sophisticated conversations to frenetic,

(Three Days of the Condor)

Researcher Joe Turner (Robert Redford) in front of the CIA office, which has been disguised as the American Literary Historical Society. *(Three Days of the Condor)*

the audience then learn that Cross has truly been a double-agent, that his wife knew all along and that she acted as a "cut-out" for a Czech courier who turns out to be Scorpio's lover. He eventually guns her and Cross down, and as the film ends Scorpio is last seen in the cross hairs of another professional's gunsight.

Although criticized by *Variety* for its cultured dialogue, *Scorpio's* conversations gave the film its uniquely complex political coloration. Burt Lancaster gave his character the air of a worldly wise cynic whose ties to the Russians were as mercenary as they were emotional. With three separate bank accounts totalling more than a quarter of a million dollars, Cross's dismissal of Zharkov's Communist faith had a firm basis. Yet, Cross had all the earmarks of the 1930's leftist liberal. The whistled "Internationale," the reference to Spain, the twenty-year friendship with Zharkov, his obvious affection for Max and Cross's contacts among Washington, D.C. area Blacks were all hints of his real political sympathies. His warnings to Scorpio were justified, and Cross's treason seemed minor compared to the CIA's criminal behavior. The traditional reference points, affection for his wife and friends, all proclaimed Cross's guiltlessness, and in fact, the CIA stood more condemned in the film. There was even a studied similarity in the names of the fictional CIA chief and its real director, McCone. If it hadn't been for its irregular pacing, the juxtaposition

Jobert (center, Max Von Sydow) closes the door as his two gunmen (left, Jay Devlin and Hank Garrett) start to work. *(Three Days of the Condor)*

Having called the CIA message center, Turner (Robert Redford) ponders his next move. *(Three Days of the Condor)*

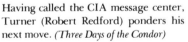

Joe Turner (Robert Redford) discovers the corpses of his colleagues when he returns from an unnoticed lunch break. *(Three Days of the Condor)*

99

Fearful of going home, Turner (Robert Redford) catches the name of a customer at a ski-wear shop. *(Three Days of the Condor)*

"I work for the CIA—I'm not a spy; I just read books," Turner tells an incredulous Katharine (Faye Dunaway). *(Three Days of the Condor)*

Hearing her name called, Katharine (Faye Dunaway) will soon meet Turner (Robert Redford). *(Three Days of the Condor)*

of slow, talky scenes with far too gymnastic thriller sequences, *Scorpio* might have been a domestic *The Spy Who Came in from the Cold.* The spy film that did eventually serve this role appeared in 1975, *Three Days of the Condor.*

Coming in the wake of the sensational disclosures about the Presidential abuse of the CIA and FBI during the Watergate break-in, *Three Days of the Condor* featured the story of an innocent victim cast amid the lions and scorpions released by the spy masters. Joe Turner (Robert Redford) was CIA reader–researcher whose codename gave the film its title. Turner's job was to read spy novels in various languages for clues to actual espionage networks unknown to the CIA's giant computer. Not at all trained for the "field," Turner is horrified to return from a back-door lunch break to find all his colleagues in the American Literary Historical Society murdered. When a meeting with a presumably friendly superior turns into a gun fight, Tur-

Incredulous and terrified, Katharine (Faye Dunaway) appears the pure image of the innocent victim caught in the spy network. *(Three Days of the Condor)*

ner is both confused and worried that his own CIA bosses are trying to kill him. The CIA chieftains, Wabash and Higgins (John Houseman and Cliff Robertson), for their part, are quite ready to accept Condor as a murderous traitor or to use him as the bait to snare the actual murderer. Part of their suspicion is fed by Condor's apparent ability to second-guess his assailants and to conduct himself like an experienced agent; the reason was simple and

An appropriately suspicious Turner (right, Robert Redford) hesitates to turn his back on his companion in the elevator, Jobert (Max Von Sydow). *(Three Days of the Condor)*

became one of the film's jokes—Condor read about spies, everything about them!

As if one innocent victim were not enough, Sidney Pollack's film has a second

Wicks (Michael Kane) takes aim at an unsuspecting Turner (Robert Redford) during a scheduled rendezvous. *(Three Days of the Condor)*

Although he cannot shoot, Jobert (Max Von Sydow) does use the telescopic sight to read Turner's license plate. *(Three Days of the Condor)*

Katharine (Faye Dunaway) helps Turner (Robert Redford) out. *(Three Days of the Condor)*

quasi-amateur spy, Kathy (Faye Dunaway), a woman forced at gunpoint by Condor to hide him, since he needs someone totally unknown to his CIA employers. Initially skeptical, she soon comes to believe his story of spies and assassins, while Wabash and Higgins are trying to determine who was actually behind the machine-gunning of a relatively innocu-

ous research unit. Turner's reading, however, has not been completely harmless, since he has hit upon traces of an espionage network operating in the Near East, a spy organization headed by one of Wabash's fellow-CIA directors. To silence Condor and his entire unit, they have hired Jobert (Max Von Sydow), an Alsatian assassin who very nearly accomplishes his mission, until assigned a bigger contract to murder his former employer. So

The postman (Hank Garrett) dispatched by Jobert grapples with Turner (Robert Redford) in Katharine's living room. *(Three Days of the Condor)*

Redford and Dunaway filming the romantic scene for *Three Days of the Condor*. (Note Klieg light in background.)

building, having disclosed the full story of the clique within the CIA which nearly killed him. As a prescient Higgins leaves Condor on the sidewalk, the direct implication is that Condor's truthful disclosure might not be printed, would change nothing if it were and would definitely signal the accident about which Jobert had warned him.

Three Days of the Condor had links to *The 39 Steps* and *The Spy Who Came in from the Cold.* An amateur hurled by intrigue and circumstances into a duel-to-the-death with mysterious foes, Turner, like Hannay before him, had to rely on the help of an incredulous woman. Like Alec Leamas, however, Joe Turner experienced a startling disillusionment,

impressed by Condor's skill, for a novice, Jobert warns his young colleague that though he has survived this incident, in two or three years an accident could occur, and he advises Condor to leave for Europe and to go into business for himself. When questioned about causes or motives, Jobert proclaims that the only worthwhile cause is the belief in one's own precision.

The Alsatian's warning takes on a deeper meaning and wider ramifications when Condor confronts Higgins to demand the explanation for the murder of so many people and the "Company's" use of him as a decoy. Higgins' major concern, however, is the protection of "the intelligence community" from strategic plans and schemes that get out of hand, like the one which Condor uncovered, and he seems unconcerned over the deaths involved. Sickened by such cynicism, Condor is last seen in front of *The New York Times*

Turner (Robert Redford) finally kills his would-be assassin. (*Three Days of the Condor*)

Mr. Wabash (John Houseman), CIA director in *Three Days of the Condor*, must determine Turner's real role.

Deputy New York Director for the CIA, R. Higgins (Cliff Robertson), rests behind his desk. *(Three Days of the Condor)*

Katharine (Faye Dunaway) escorts a worried Higgins (center, Cliff Robertson) to a waiting Turner (Robert Redford). *(Three Days of the Condor)*

Turner (Robert Redford) and Katharine (Faye Dunaway) discuss the next move in their personal espionage war. *(Three Days of the Condor)*

since the organization for which he worked, for which his friends died and for which he unearthed an internal threat looked upon him as a potential traitor, an unwanted success. That threat may have been "sanitized," stripped of any real significance, since the plot he uncovered was not an official or routine CIA operation. No matter how blandly conceived, the idea of a murderous group working within the CIA reverberated well beyond the movie theater ticket office.

Senators and congressmen had already clashed over the CIA's role in formulating national policy even before the Watergate break-in. Books detailing the clandestine activities of CIA men in Latin America and Southeast Asia had become best sellers, and college students had begun to picket CIA recruiters on their local campuses. In a series of press conferences and scandals worthy of a Frank Launder screenplay, one Agency representative boasted of the high number of PhD's among its employees, and various universities admitted having research funds larded with CIA money. The Justice Department and the Supreme Court clashed over the strength of re- strictions on wiretapping and eavesdropping devices, while the State Department worried about their ambassadors' inability to control or even know of CIA operations abroad.

A part of the conflict was purely political —who was to determine the aims of American spies and who was to control their methods— while another part was historical. The wartime practices and styles, the cloak-and-dagger exploits of the Office of Strategic Services in occupied Europe, had not been applicable to Eastern Europe or Soviet Russia. While sophisticated and highly sensitive equipment was aimed at the Russians, flown over the Chinese mainland or placed in orbit over Cuba, the exponents of palace coups and secret armies sought and found fertile terrain in the underdeveloped nations of the Third World, in Africa, Asia and Latin America. For many spies in both the CIA and KGB the postwar world lacked the easy recognizability of friends and enemies; they were like Cross and Zharkov, or Diego and Leamas, Happy and Kurt Muller; they needed the real possibility of war to give their lives and work real meaning.

Turner (Robert Redford) threatens CIA leader Leonard Atwood (Addison Powell) to obtain information. *(Three Days of the Condor)*

4

The Possibility of War

While the baroness (Mary Clare) watches their train disappear, a curiously benign Dr. Hartz (Paul Lukas) wishes his escaped quarry good luck. *(The Lady Vanishes)*

The Lady Vanishes
Confessions of a Nazi Spy
Foreign Correspondent
The Seventh Cross
Across the Pacific
The Invaders (The 49th Parallel)
The House on 92nd Street

Unlike its generic cousins, the cowboy and gangster film, the espionage feature did not focus on the capture of the frontier town's marauders or the city crime bosses, but on the victory of a nation and its values in a war that was seen as imminent. The spy or, more accurately, the counterspy, was the personal embodiment of the nation in a clash that received little or no public recognition until well after the event. Just as actual spies were sent out long in advance of the invading armies, the spy films were often harbingers of the war that many people were already reading about in their daily newspapers. Besides being presentiments of war, the films also gauged popular opinion and sang the praises of national character in a situation that was not only dangerous but increasingly relevant. In the years preceding the war, spy films could not only pit conscious adversaries against each other, but could also use heroic bystanders and innocent victims to underline the moral that the impending war concerned everybody. The spy film could serve as an allegory, and one of the films that played consciously with the theme of

European dictatorships and a war was Alfred Hitchcock's *The Lady Vanishes.*

Made in 1938, a year ideally suited for allegory, which had opened with the German absorption of Austria, was to end with the dismemberment of Czechoslovakia and was echoed throughout by the Spanish Civil War and the Japanese attack on China, *The Lady Vanishes* climaxed with a border clash between secret police and a band of English tourists. The film's opening introduces us to a group of British travellers stranded in what one of them describes as "a third-rate hotel in a third-rate country." Even the pair of cinematically type-cast middle-class Englishmen, Caldicott and Charters (Naunton Wayne and Basil Radford), forget their continual concern over cricket to help fight off the secret police. The film's dialogue, written by Frank Launder and Sydney Gilliat, is replete with gently ironic references to various English character traits and prejudices. The cricket fans are initially seen and heard fretting over the current "crisis" facing England, a crisis which sounds ominously political until the revelatory punch

Mrs. Froy (Dame May Whitty) leaves a message with the Bandriekan hotel manager, Boris (Emile Boreo). *(The Lady Vanishes)*

line about the cricket test matches in Manchester. Even the actual spy, Mrs. Froy (Dame May Whitty), whose disappearance gives the film its title, avoids the word spy, stating, "It's so grim, don't you think," and has as her cover the eminently respectable and typically English position of governess and music teacher.

The major protagonists are also typically Anglo-Saxon types cast into a mysterious situation: Gilbert (Michael Redgrave), a wandering Cambridge musicologist collecting folk tunes, and Iris Henderson (Margaret Lockwood), a wealthy American heiress engaged to an English aristocrat. All these characters express some form of condescension towards Bandrieka, the country in which they find themselves stranded, although both Gilbert's and Mrs. Froy's attitudes are mitigated by amiability and the ability to speak the language. More importantly, it is the English passengers assembled for high tea in the dining car to whom Gilbert appeals for help when the secret police attack the train. Even the enemy spy who unexpectedly helps them does so because of her reluctance to kill a fellow countrywoman.

The characters in the besieged train typify the expected reactions to an armed fight: the cricket enthusiasts, Caldicott and Charters, calmly return the enemy's fire, while the pompous and adulterous barrister, Todhunter (Cecil Parker), makes an unsuccessful bid

Growing suspicious, Iris Henderson (Margaret Lockwood) eyes her travel companions, while Gilbert (Michael Redgrave) holds her bag. *(The lady Vanishes)*

A distraught Iris (Margaret Lockwood) hears a somber diagnosis from Dr. Hartz (right, Paul Lukas), while Gilbert (left, Michael Redgrave) comforts her and a suspicious steward looks on. *(The Lady Vanishes)*

for peace and dies waving a white handkerchief. A skillful piece of melodramatic allegory, Hitchcock's twenty-fourth film had been constructed out of the familiar ingredients of innocents caught up in a complicated intrigue. Once again there was the introduction of apparently innocuous events that advanced the story and developed the plot: the street guitarist and the musical Mrs. Froy, the cricket fans and their reluctance to impede their return home, the adulterous Todhunters and their fear of scandal, and the whimsical Gilbert and his light-hearted willingness to help Iris in her search for Mrs. Froy. The duel of wits between the Anglo-Americans, Gilbert and Iris, and the Continental spies, Dr. Hartz (Paul Lu-

kas) and the Baroness (Mary Claire), was buttressed by frequent references to Bandrieka's dictatorship, especially by Caldicott and Charters.

The Lady Vanishes, however, was not an explicit political allegory. Bandrieka first appeared on the screen as an obvious scale model set with snow-covered miniature houses and cars, while the visual hints at dictatorship were closer to operetta than to the Third Reich. Despite these features the location and timing of this film was much closer to the grim realities of Europe than *The 39 Steps.* Other filmmakers were also interested in the impending war and were not willing to operate within the confines of a fictional espionage

The English Passengers: the Todhunters (left, Cecil Parker and Linden Travers), Gilbert (Michael Redgrave), Caldicott (Naunton Wayne), and Charters (Basil Radford) aid the defecting agent disguised as a nun (Catherine Lacey), while Iris (Margaret Lockwood) and Mrs. Froy (right, Dame May Whitty) look on. *(The Lady Vanishes)*

Nazi emissary Schlager (left, George Sanders) contemptuously eyes his new agent, while Curt Schneider (Francis Lederer) looks at the German's bulging billfold. *(Confessions of a Nazi Spy)*

narrator, Reed Hadley, to link fictional scenes with occasional newsreel sequences. Litvak and his screen writers, Milton Krims and John Wexley, dramatized the extensive, if amateur, spy apparatus lurking within the German-American organizations that aped the Nazi Party in style and tone. As well as illustrating the espionage attempts by the zealots of the German-American Bund, *Confessions of a Nazi Spy* also highlighted the personal psychopathology which led them to become agents.

Curt Schneider (Francis Lederer) was depicted as a frustrated and unemployed husband, tormented by his wife's criticism, their modest standard of living and his desire to be a "big shot." Inflamed by the speakers at the Bund meetings he faithfully attends, Schneider writes to the German Naval Intelligence Headquarters in Berlin to offer his services as a spy. Astounded by Schneider's blunt offer, the German naval officers forward his request to the relevant Nazi Party office and in this way Curt Schneider is given a relatively minor intelligence-gathering task to test his skill and loyalty. Asked to determine the strength of the regiments in the New York City region, Schneider impersonates an army medical officer over the phone to get the weekly hospital reports from which he can extrapolate the actual numerical figures. His success attracts the attention of a Nazi spy organizer, Schlager (George Sanders), whose imperious manner

plot with carefully delineated characters. In Hollywood Anatole Litvak made a 1939 film treating the problem of Nazi espionage in America as it had been revealed by an earlier Federal investigation.

Litvak's *Confessions of a Nazi Spy* used a quasi-documentary format with a voice-over

At an outdoor *Bund* rally, Dr. Kassel (Paul Lukas), flanked by two Gestapo men sent from Berlin, Hintze (left, Lionel Royce) and Helldorf (Henry Victor), addresses his followers. *(Confessions of a Nazi Spy)*

and measly payment of fifty dollars disappoints Schneider, who had to fulfill Schlager's request for several blank American passports. Schneider has also attracted the attention of FBI Inspector Renard (Edward G. Robinson).

Alerted by Scotland Yard, which has discovered the postal "cut-out" between Berlin and its American agents, all the U.S. letters have been diverted to Renard who immediately sees that he is dealing not with a professional spy, but a "Hitler happy" amateur, a Bund member eager to work for the Fatherland. Part of the film's emphasis was on preparedness for war; one of the government officials conferring with Renard complains that his office for counter-intelligence has only one man in New York City to keep track of potential enemy spies. As the counterpoint to this theme is the re-creation of Nazi style Bund meetings and summer camp rallies where Bund leader, Dr. Kassel (Paul Lukas), and Schlager admire the marching of the youth members in their *Hitler Jugend* uniforms. The film, however, has a curious ambivalence: despite Schneider's grandiose posturing, his only success is the procurement of the regimental figures, and Kassel's sychophantic imitation of Hitler's speaking style at the Bund meetings contrasts with his healthy fear of Schlager and his subordinates. Schlager and his troupe of Gestapo men are ready to stiffen and discipline their American agents'

resolve. The tension between the German Nazis and their American apprentices is seen when Bund members who had begun to doubt the wisdom of importing Nazism into the United States are forcibly repatriated aboard the same passenger liner that ferried Schlager and his lieutenants between Hamburg and New York.

The psychology of the various spies played an important part in the film, since it was by cleverly playing on their personality traits that Renard was able to build his case against them. Flattering Schneider with praise for his skill and importance as a German agent, Renard is able to get detailed information about Schneider's crimes and then threatens him with severe punishment unless he reveals the names of his bosses and colleagues. Kassel was depicted as a typical Germanic *untertan*, an underling who bullied those below him and groveled before his superiors, whether Schlager or Renard. There was also a personal aspect to Kassel's plight, since his wife, aware of his marital infidelity, deliberately lets him walk into a trap set by Schlager to punish him for his cooperation with the FBI. Kassel had agreed to testify for the prosecution at the trial, so that he ends up being shipped back to Germany without any of the fanfare granted him on an earlier visit. As part of that pilgrimage a gloating and sleek Dr. Goebbels (Martin Kosleck) had outlined

FBI Inspector Ed Renard (center, Edward G. Robinson) arrests one of the Nazi spies, Hilda (Dorothy Tree) while FBI man Phillips (Fred Tozere) looks on. *(Confessions of a Nazi Spy)*

Dr. Kassel (right, Paul Lukas) proudly shows his files on racial genealogy to an incredulous FBI agent, Ed Renard (Edward G. Robinson). *(Confessions of a Nazi Spy)*

Nazi plans for conquest and had reminded Kassel to dress National Socialism in American colors but never to forget that Nazism was the hammer and not the anvil.

Confessions of a Nazi Spy had a shrillness of tone attributable to the depiction of its enemy agents as Nazi ideologues. Kassel proudly showed the visiting Renard his files on the racial genealogy of Americans prominent in business and government. The support given the Bund members was depicted in similarly emotional terms when the visual sequences illustrated the voice-over discussion of the massive shipments of propaganda literature smuggled into North and South America by German freighters. The film ended, as it had begun, with a courtroom scene where the District Attorney (Henry O'Neill) is delivering an impassioned summation to the jury, and of course the viewing audience, about the importance of fighting the new kind of undeclared war being waged in America. A commercial and critical success, this film not only confirmed Warner Brothers as the preeminent socially oriented studio in Hollywood, but also introduced American feature film audiences, *the* mass of miviegoers, to the topical drama rewritten from actual events and employing newsreel footage within its staged sequences.

Part of the film's success had to do with reality, since a year before its release there had been a series of federal investigations and trials of Nazi sympathizers and organizers. *Confessions of a Nazi Spy* triggered a German diplomatic counter-offensive which succeeded in having the film banned in some eighteen countries.

Events, however, moved even faster and surer than the FBI's Renard; the shooting war began in Europe, so that the film was re-released with newsreel footage to include the invasion of Poland and Anglo-French declarations of war. More important changes were needed for the cinematic spies than additional dialogue and footage; there were now no longer any really innocent bystanders. The *Wehrmacht's* advance into Poland had stripped away the need for allegories or mythic overlays, except for the finer sensibilities of an American film industry that was officially neutral for two more years. For one more allegory about the prewar period, United artists turned to that seasoned professional, Alfred Hitchcock. *Foreign Correspondent* was dedicated to the international reporters "who early saw the clouds of war," and the idea for the production, Hitchcock has told interviewers, stemmed from a well-known journalist's autobiography. Although dedicated to reporters,

Spy master Krug (left, Eduardo Cian-nelli) discusses with one of his henchmen the fate of the drugged Van Meer (center, Albert Bassermann). *(Foreign Correspondent)*

the film was almost a cinematic complement to Evelyn Waugh's *Scoop,* a satirical novel about a reporter assigned to cover an African civil war.

The title star, Johnny Jones, (Joel Mc-Crea), a city crime reporter, is initially seen seated behind his desk cutting paper dolls, since he expects to be fired for having slugged a cop. It is this act, however, which earns him an assignment to Europe, since, combined with his acknowledged indifference and ignorance of the European crisis, he is, in the publisher's view, a "fresh, unused mind." Looking for a writer who doesn't know the "difference between an ism and a kangaroo," publisher Powers (Harry Davenport) sends his Ameri-

A suitably attired Johnny Jones (left, Joel McCrea) is about to discover the kidnapped statesman Van Meer (Albert Bassermann). *(Foreign Correspondent)*

Jones (left, Joel McCrea) and Scott Ffoliott (George Sanders) try to think up a
plan to ensnare Van Meer's kidnappers.
(*Foreign Correspondent*)

can innocent abroad. (Hitchcock has said that he would have preferred Gary Cooper for the role, but at the time spy films and thrillers were considered "B" films unworthy of the prime players.) As Jones, McCrea fell into the sequence of events common to so many Hitchcock films: the mixture of luck and conspiracy that surrounds his heroic victims. Assigned to interview the Dutch pacifist-statesman, Van Meer (Albert Bassermann), Jones accompanies him to a luncheon in his honor which the man mysteriously misses. Later a Van Meer who doesn't seem to recognize or remember Jones is assassinated on the staircase leading to a special Dutch pacifist meeting, and Jones is suspicious not only of the murder but of the assassin's disappearance as well.

Van Meer was the "MacGuffin" in this film, while the background was Europe on the brink of war; the crisis joked about in *The Lady Vanishes* had become serious. Jones' apathy towards the crisis and his cynicism about the peace movement could be seen as typical American attitudes coverted in the course of

the film by the Van Meer incident and Jones' love for Carol Fisher (Laraine Day), a pacifist organizer. Her father, Stephen (Herbert Marshall), the leader of the pacifist organization and a close friend of Van Meer's is, in reality, a German spy working in league with the more outwardly ominous Krug (Eduardo Cianelli), to discover the clauses to a secret Belgian–Dutch treaty. A witness to the fact that the real Van Meer is a live hostage in Krug's hands, Jones has become a threat and the next target of the conspiracy. Fortunately for Jones, not only has Carol fallen in love with him, but he also has a guardian in the form of Herbert Ffoliott (George Sanders), an English reporter with apparent links to Scotland Yard and the Secret Service. Not only has Ffoliott suspected for some time that Fisher is a German agent, but he also supports Jones in his attempt to rescue Van Meer. Sanders traditionally played enemy roles in most espionage films; his part in *Foreign Correspondent* was only a minor example of casting-against-type, best exemplified in this film by Edmund Gwenn in the role

While the Filipino assassin (Rudy Robles) takes a bead on Dr. Lorenz (Sydney Greenstreet), "Rick" Leland (Humphrey Bogart) already has the would-be patriot covered. (*Across the Pacific*)

more than a touch of military bearing. Both to win Lorenz's confidence and to carry out his assignment Leland has to protect the spy from a Filipino assassin whose execution he witnesses on a darkened New York wharf.

Seen by Lorenz as a frustrated and cynical military man, Leland appeared the ideal recruit who knew something about artillery and specifically the artillery placements around the Panama Canal Zone. The Japanese attack on the canal, planned to coincide with the attack on Pearl Harbor, was to have been launched from a nearby plantation owned by Dan Morton (Monte Blue), Lorenz's unwilling alcoholic host, and his daughter Alberta (Mary Astor), whom Leland has met on board the freighter. Leland, of course, single-handedly foils the plot in the scene that was to become standard for Hollywood wartime films. Wearing the famous Bogart grimace, Leland machine-guns down a small army of disguised spies and soldiers on the plantation who come charging at his captured machine gun. The characterization of Leland as a professional soldier explains his skill and success, while an interesting comment is drawn from Bogart's persona as a performer. The distraught Lor-

enz, faced with the failure of his mission, has been unable to perform his ritual suicide and asks Leland to shoot him. Whether as a sarcastic comment on the villain's Japanophilia or as conscious tribute to Bogart's famous role as

Publicity photograph of Humphrey Bogart and Mary Astor for *Across the Pacific*.

Duke Mantee in *The Petrified Forest,* the good lieutenant refuses.

Set in the period immediately before the war, *Across the Pacific,* with its unambiguous reference to Japan in its title, established the careful clandestine preparations by which the enemy scored his major victories and the skill needed to defeat him. With the combined merits of screenplay, direction and performance, the idea was conveyed to audiences that a good double-agent must not wear his heart on his sleeve and must be willing to make the enemy believe they are traitors or indifferent to politics, as in the case of the doomed Filipino assassin. This personal resolve was the topic of another 1942 film that focused not on espionage preparations but on the individual reconciliation with the fact of a war with a determined antagonist who posed a very real threat even to peaceful citizens with little real interest in the conflict—*The 49th Parallel,* also known to television viewers as *The Invaders.*

This Michael Powell and Emeric Pressburger film was not technically about spies, but about a number of German U-boat officers and men stranded on Canadian soil after their boat is sighted and sunk by RCAF aircraft. Even before their mishap the Germans have been depicted as a heartless bunch who have gleefully filmed the crew of a Canadian ship they have just torpedoed but have refused them food and water. Once stranded on enemy soil, their leader, a Lieutenant Hirth (Eric Portman), shows a singular ruthlessness, while his colleague, a less Nazified engineer, Lieutenant Kunecke (Raymond Lovell), applies his intelligence without scruple to Hirth's orders and the other ranks vacillate between firm obedience and wavering doubts. The film's contrast and drama emerged from the confrontation of Canadian civilians with the U-boat men. Hirth tries to convince the French-Canadian trapper, Jonnie, (Laurence Olivier), that Nazism could help him and his people, but the politically indifferent Quebecker soon learns first-hand about Nazism when he makes an abortive attempt to radio for help. The Germans, however, are not totally successful; one Nazi is shot by an Eskimo marks-

Crew member of the torpedoed freighter *Anticostolite* (a non-professional recruited from among Newfoundland fishermen) is being filmed by one of the U-boat's officers. *(The 49th Parallel [also known as The Invaders])*

man and another dies in the crash of their stolen plane. Perhaps the most interesting episode is the defection of one of the seamen, Vogel (Niall MacGinnis).

Hunting for shelter the U-boat men come across a German-speaking Hutterite farming commune. In a sequence that is saved from near absurdity by Portman's performance, Hirth mistakes the Hutterites' spartan, rural creed for a North American version of National Socialism and his Hitlerite speech to them is a complete fiasco, besides angering the Hutterite leader, Peter (Anton Walbrook), and the farm girl who has befriended them, Anna (Glynis Johns). Hirth's failure is mirrored, in reverse, by Vogel, who has found a happy solace as the comune's baker, a return to his peacetime occupation. Swayed by Peter's acceptance of him and his own guilt over the fact that Anna's mother had died in a torpedo attack on the ship bringing her to Canada, Vogel refuses to join the other Nazi in their trek towards a still neutral United States. For this he is condemned as a deserter and traitor and shot by Hirth. One more U-boat man has died in Canada and this time at the hands of his countrymen and crew members.

The Nazi odyssey continues after this confrontation with the other German tradi-

Lieutenants Hirth (left, Eric Portman) and Kuhnecke (right, Raymond Lovell) flank their men as they all salute the dawn over Hudson's Bay. *(The 49th Parallel)*

tion until faced with contemporary English values, personified in the character of a writer, Phillip Armstrong Scott, played by none other than Leslie Howard. Scott thinks the forlorn pair some lost vacationers and offers them food and lodging. Hirth looks upon his kindness and generosity as softness and deca-

dence, a belief bolstered by Scott's taste for Picasso and Thomas Mann. When they reveal themselves as the U-boat men for whom the Canadian authorities have been searching, the two men not only lecture Scott on the superiority of the Nazi way of life, they also destroy his manuscript, paintings and books as an ob-

German sailor making sure none of the *Anticostolite's* survivors try to board the U-37. *(The 49th Parallel)*

121

Lieutenant Hirth (center, Eric Portman) orders the Hudson's Bay Trading Company factor (right, Finlay Currie) about, while Lohrmann (left, John Chandos) stands ready to enforce those orders. (*The 49th Parallel*)

ject lesson. Scott, of course, gets his revenge, when alone and unarmed he faces down and knocks out one of the Nazis holed up in a cave. Hirth, however, is still free, the object of both a Canadian manhunt and a German propaganda campaign which hails him as the Nazi conqueror of Canada. As the German radio announcer fades from the screen, Hirth appears hidden in the freight compartment of a train nearing the American border. Soon to join him is an AWOL Canadian soldier, Andy Brock (Raymond Massey), whose complaints Hirth takes for serious political disaffection. When Hirth tries to steal his uniform for the

Lieutenant Hirth (right, Eric Portman) tells the Hutterite farmers about National Socialism, without much success. (*The 49th Parallel*)

A remorseful U-boat sailor, Vogel (left, Niall McGinnis), asks Peter (Anton Walbrook) if he could stay as the community's baker. *(The 49th Parallel)*

passage across the border, Brock has both the excuse and opportunity to fight a real live Nazi without leaving Canada.

The 49th Parallel was made during the war and used it as the background to its story, but the film's strength and success lay in the contrast between pacific spirits like Jonnie and Phillip Scott and the aggressive German lieu-

tenant, and the change in the Canadians' attitudes. Conceived as a film in 1940, production relied on the talents of some of the English industry's most prestigious stars and had to be scheduled according to their availability. The only criticism the film received revolved around the portrayal of the Germans as competent and determined enemies who could

Hirth (left, Eric Portman) and Lohrmann (right, John Chandos) repay Philip Armstrong Scott (center, Leslie Howard) for his hospitality. *(The 49th Parallel)*

AWOL canadian army trooper Andy Brock (right, Raymond Massey) will soon discover how close the enemy, Hirth (Eric Portman), can be in wartime. *(The 49th Parallel)*

not be minimized nor laughed away, except perhaps at the film's close. Another film which depicted the enemy on "our" soil was both a traditional espionage film and something of a landmark in cinematic history, Louis de Rochemont's *The House on 92nd Street.*

Directed by Henry Hathaway in 1945, this film not only detailed an actual case of German espionage, it also set the tone and style for a number of spy films dealing with both wartime and postwar themes. Filmed almost entirely on location in New York City

and replete with laboratory and office footage supplied by the FBI, Rochemont's production achieved a remarkable similarity to a documentary despite the use of such familiar performers as Lloyd Nolan, Leo G. Carroll, Signe Hasso and Gene Lockhart.

The plot concerned a young German-American, Bill Dietrich (William Eythe), who had been contacted while a college student by German agents to become a spy. Sent to Germany before the war to receive specialized training, Dietrich has already notified the FBI

Spies, civil defense, and the war linked to *The Invaders (The 49th Parallel)* in this book display.

124

Veteran German Spy Colonel Hammersohn (left, Leo G. Carroll) makes sure Bill Dietrich (William Eythe) realizes the importance of his assignment. *(The House on 92nd Street)*

and is working as a double-agent when the film's action starts. Supplied by the FBI with a doctored directive from his German superiors, Dietrich manages to meet all the spies controlled by the resident of the film title's address, Elsa Gebhardt (Signe Hasso). These spies include both standard heavies like Max (Harry Belaver), and Conrad (Harro Meller), as well as the experienced trained professional, Colonel Hammersohn (Leo G. Carroll). By means of movie cameras behind one-way mirrors and Dietrich's devious ways of avoiding his erstwhile colleagues, for example, driving on the wrong lane on the George Washington bridge, FBI Inspector Briggs (Lloyd Nolan) and the audience could follow the pro-

Bill Dietrich (third from left, William Eythe) receives instructions in cryptography from the *Abwehr's* specialists. *(The House on 92nd Street)*

While Gestapo liaison Joanna Schmidt (right, Lydia St. Clair) keeps watch, Walker (left, William Post, Jr.) discloses shipping information to Dietrich (right, William Eythe) and Adolf Klaen (Alfred Lindner). *(The House on 92nd Street)*

gress of the deception. Even Dietrich's radio transmissions to Hamburg were screened through a special relaying station, and it is this trick that betrays Dietrich since Conrad realizes at a glance that Dietrich's own radio equipment couldn't possibly reach Europe.

The film's essentially episodic structure was held together by a familiar off-screen voice, Reed Hadley, and the suspense surrounding a mysterious German agent, Mr. Christopher, who had the authority to alter all instructions. Initially only the name on the lips of a dying German spy killed in a car accident, Mr. Christopher is seen by the audience only occassionally in close-up shots of the familiar shoes and spats that signified Christopher's presence. It was only at the film's close that Christopher was seen as an appropriately attired Signe Hasso.

The film displayed many of the technical details of spycraft without too much melodrama: microdots under postage stamps, ap-

To avoid being followed by the Nazi spies, Dietrich (William Eythe) lets himself be arrested for a traffic violation. *(The House on 92nd Street)*

FBI Inspector Briggs (Lloyd Nolan) receiving news of the German spies' activities. *(The House on 92nd Street)*

parently routine customs inspections to mask important exchanges and the importance of business-like covers. The only major flaw in *The House on 92nd Street* lay in Dietrich's characterization: there was little room in the screenplay for much evidence of Dietrich's motivations or emotions, no expression of his fears and tensions as a double-agent, perhaps the most dangerous of counter-espionage tasks. The villains, Elsa Gebhardt and Colonel Hammersohn, emerged as the film's most interesting characters, particularly the elegant

Colonel, a veteran spy from the First World War, whose irony and expertise eclipsed both Dietrich and the FBI camera team filming them from behind a one-way glass. There were also elements of apparent imitation in this conscious quasi-documentary. One of the lesser German agents, we learn from Inspector Briggs, had been a hairdresser on a North German Lloyd passenger ship, and in *Confessions of a Nazi Spy,* one of the sequences involved the use of a ship's beautician as an informer. Another hint of an earlier film lay in

127

To investigate the house on 92nd Street, Inspector Briggs (left, Lloyd Nolan) has his agents pose as Civil Defense inspectors. *(The House on 92nd Street)*

FBI agent about to take book dealer and contact, Adolf Lang (Bruno Wick), in for questioning. *(The House on 92nd Street)*

the identity of the agent passing atomic research secrets to the Germans, Ogden Roper (Gene Lockhart), a clerk responsible for photographing scientific documents. Roper, FBI investigation reveals near the film's end, had once been a music hall performer whose talent was a photographic memory, a skill familiar from the days of *The 39 Steps*.

Released in 1945, *The House on 92nd Street* was made with the cooperation of, and even a guest appearance at one point by, FBI Director J. Edgar Hoover. It was quite possible that the politically astute Hoover favored the idea of giving his bureau both some favorable publicity after the fact and as a warning to any

potential spies and saboteurs. Unlike earlier preparedness spy features, there was little flag-waving of either the red-white-and-blue or swastika banners. The emphasis, instead, was on the detailed, patient professionalism of the counterspy who had penetrated the enemy network. Although war was declared at one point in the film's story, the only effect was to heighten Gebhardt's and Hammersohn's caution and of course Dietrich's danger. War, however, was the final test of a spy's competence, as well as the logic by which governmental needs and decisions superseded the emotions and often the lives of its own agents.

Inspector Briggs (Lloyd Nolan) questions Frieda Kassel (Elisabeth Neumann). *(The House on 92nd Street)*

5

The Intricacies of War

U-boat captain Hardt (Conrad Veidt) and the British schoolmistress (Valerie Hobson) pose in this publicity still from *The Spy in Black*.

The Spy in Black
Five Graves to Cairo
Cloak and Dagger
The Man Who Never Was
The Counterfeit Traitor

Once the war had been declared and become a matter of public concern, the spy film could explore the technical execution of either simple or elaborate plots with all the necessary military details and graphic violence. There could be somber scenes of generals and statesmen seated around felt-covered tables discussing the strategic importance of the spy mission soon to unfold on the screen, as well as imposing shots of the Luftwaffe air base, Nazi secret weapons laboratory or Hitler headquarters against which the Allied spies were sent. With one or two exceptions most English and American espionage features depicted purely defensive operations against the wartime foe; the Allied agents were seen at work only after the war had started, unlike the Axis spies who were seen busily planning for war years before the first shell burst. The best wartime spy films did not minimize the dangers and difficulties of wartime espionage on enemy occupied soil, since like the good suspense and adventure variants the antagonists must not be depicted as simple pushovers. The importance of the enemy's characterization also stemmed from a

popular thirst for information, particularly concerning the psychology of the German and Japanese aggressors. As a matter of film history, Hollywood churned out a number of wartime films set in Nazi Germany to answer this need and to attempt some explanation, no matter how simple-minded, of Nazism's hold over the German people. Although many of the wartime spy films did provide entertaining and insightful comments, most were painfully mediocre.

In far too many films the reliance on typecast characters whose obviousness was mirrored by secret rooms festooned with Hitler portraits and swastika banners, radio transmitters and military maps was the rule. Discovered within the film's first quarter-hour, the remaining three-quarters was devoted to their effortless defeat and capture. The Allied spy in Germany was conversely always able to evade the teams of appropriately uniformed Gestapo men with Doberman pinschers or shepherd dogs which searched the same studio sets in film after film. Wartime propaganda often had its demands that superseded any screenwriter's skill or director's style; both Hitchcock and Powell were criticized for drawing too formidable a picture of the enemy. As a result many of the films in this section were made after the war or near its close, and only one was made before it.

That early film was Michael Powell's 1939 *The Spy in Black,* which starred Conrad Veidt as Captain Hardt, a World War I U-boat officer whose orders took him to Scotland on a special espionage mission. Opening with a routine U-boat attack on Allied shipping, *The Spy in Black* emphasized Hardt's personality. He shared with his fellow officers their despondence over what had become a lost war and their discomfort over the rationing that limited food and substituted ersatz in its place. Ordered to spy on the Royal Navy anchored at Scapa Flow, Hardt journeys there by U-boat and overland by motorcycle; the film derived its title from the leather motorcyclist suit he wears while riding under the cover of a midnight Scottish fog bank. When Hardt meets his local contact, a schoolteacher (Valerie

Spy (Conrad Veidt) and counterspy (Valerie Hobson) take the measure of each other's feigned and real emotions. *(The Spy in Black)*

Captain Hardt (left of group, Conrad Veidt) and his officers enjoy an evening of shore leave after their U-boat mission. *(The Spy in Black)*

Supporting players Anne Burnett (June Duprez) and Ashington (Sebastian Shaw), from *The Spy in Black*.

Hobson), he stares intently not at her nor her comfortable house, but at the kitchen table where he sees a dish of real butter, and she has to correct his German pronunciation of that coveted item.

The film's action revolved around the attempt by Hardt to amass enough information about the fleet's movements to make a successful U-boat attack possible. Aiding him in this mission were the schoolmistress and Arlington (Sebastian Shaw), a cashiered naval officer who supplies information to supplement Hardt's observations from the attic window in the woman's house. She and Arlington, however, are double-agents hoping, in turn, to entrap the German attackers. Hardt has to play a complicated game of intrigue, appearing to work out the arrangements for the attack

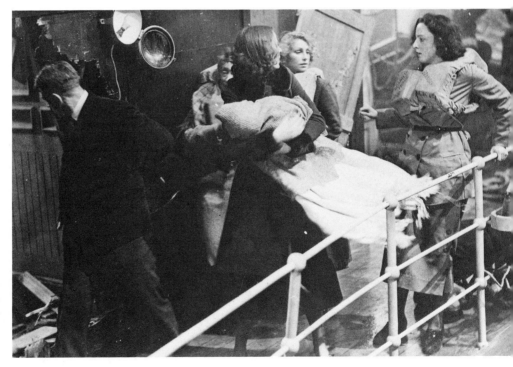

The ferry is attacked by Hardt's own U-boat; the woman trying to save the infant is the schoolmistress (Valerie Hobson). *(The Spy in Black)*

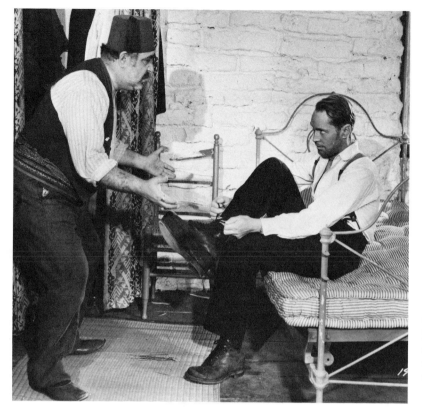

While Bramble (right, Franchot Tone) laces up Davos's corrective shoe, hotel owner Farid (Akim Tamiroff) pleads with him not to undertake the impersonation. *(Five Graves to Cairo)*

without risking capture. The film's strength lay in the subtle test of wits between the two sides, as well as the careful delineation of personalities. Hardt and the teacher were not simple combinations of various national traits; there was little flag-waving, but rather a growing mutual respect between the two spies. Much of this was due to Veidt, whose performance as the aristocratically detached naval officer spying for a government in which he had little faith nearly condemned him to play the role of enemy spies exclusively, particularly during his period in Hollywood.

The cool professionalism that suffused *The Spy in Black* appeared again only in the postwar spy films, since modern wars have de-

Mouche (Anne Baxter) distracts Bramble (Franchot Tone) from his study of an Egyptian gazeteer. *(Five Graves to Cairo)*

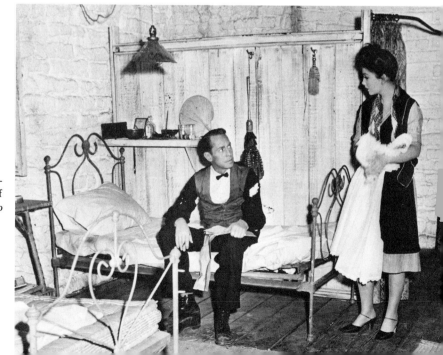

Italian General Sebastiani (Fortunio Bonanova) tells Bramble (right, Franchot Tone) how the Germans stole his toothbush. (*Five Graves to Cairo*)

manded a cinematic moralism equivalent to the passions of the medieval church. One of the wartime productions expressed its patriotism in an explanation of the initial German victories in North Africa, *Five Graves to Cairo*. Directed by Billy Wilder and scripted by Wilder in collaboration with his producer Charles Brackett and the screenwriter Lalo Biro, this film was released in early 1943 shortly after the British victory at El Alamein and incorporated some footage from that battle in its closing scenes, besides providing an imaginative explanation for that success.

A British defeat, however, opened the film, while an inter-title explained that in the summer of 1942 the *Afrika Korps* had pushed

Bramble, as Davos (center, Franchot Tone), hands a captured English officer (Miles Mander) his beret. (*Five Graves to Cairo*)

Publicity shot of Franchot Tone (1950).

the English armies far into Egypt and were threatening Alexandria and the Suez Canal. The film's story revolved around a British army corporal, J. J. Bramble (Franchot Tone), who literally stumbles onto Field Marshal Rommel's prime military secret. Dazed and exhausted, the sole survivor of a damaged lend-lease U.S. tank, Bramble staggers into a hotel, the Empress of Britain, a few minutes before German troops arrive to set up a field headquarters for the Desert Fox. The stunned Englishman lies hidden in a sideboard while Staff-Lieutenant Schwaegler (Peter Van Eyck), questions the hotel owner (Akim Tamiroff) and the chambermaid, Mouche (Anne Baxter), about the suitability of the rooms for the conquering officers. Schwaegler is depicted as an immodest victor who laughingly predicts how they would soon kill Egypt's flies as they had killed the English and gloats over the bars of English soap found in the hotel's bedrooms.

In his effort to avoid capture, and there is a distinct hint that the Germans, sparing of their water supplies, would as soon shoot him, Bramble dons a dead waiter's jacket and his corrective shoe. That waiter, Davos, an Alsatian, was apparently a German spy, since Schwaegler escorts him to an audience with His Excellency the Field Marshal (Erich von Stroheim). Piecing together bits of conversation between Rommel and Schwaegler, Bramble learns that Davos had been "an advance man who has done work in Warsaw and Amsterdam" or, as Bramble phrased it during his introduction to Rommel, "a vulture who flies before the Stukas limping a little." With this kind of access to Rommel, Bramble's idea to kill him when he rings for his breakfast is blocked by Mouche, who rushes to the Field Marshal's room with her own plan. With a disabled brother in a German POW camp, Mouche pleads with Rommel to intervene on his behalf. Disdaining to hide his contempt for "women this early in the morning," Rommel orders her several paces distant before admonishing her to write to the relevant authorities in Germany in triplicate, since "we need paper in Germany, lots of paper."

Stroheim's Rommel was a tour-de-force for the famous cinematic personality. When

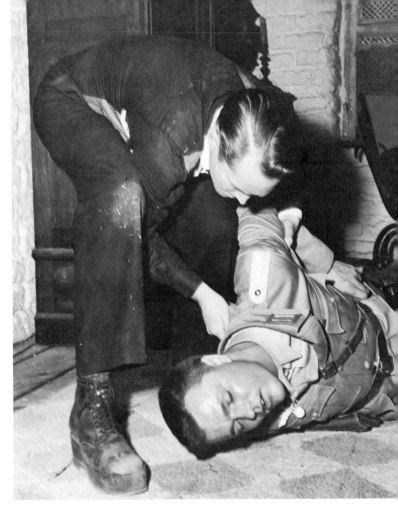

Bramble (Franchot Tone) disposing of Lieutenant Schwaegler (Peter Van Eyck). *(Five Graves to Cairo)*

first seen in an overhead tracking shot, he is dictating both in German, and, for the benefit of the enemy's intelligence service, in English, a telegram to his Fuhrer about the impending conquest of Suez. In a later, pivotal scene in which Rommel dines with several captured British officers, Stroheim's Field Marshal makes several ironic comments about both his English opponents and his Italian ally. Asked how many troops he has, Rommel truthfully responds with a grinning "not as many as you" and when asked about the Italian troops he could scornfully express what lay unspoken in many minds, that "no one counts in or on the Italians." It was the question of supplies that interested the dinner guests, particularly one officer whose exaggerated resemblance to Montgomery was one of the film's many jokes. Without fuel and water even the vaunted *Afrika Korps* would grind to a halt, and so Rommel's cryptic answer that it was not the supplies which reached him, but he who reached his supplies, was the puzzle Bramble had to solve. Bramble's only clues were Rommel's boast that the Germans had prepared for the war years before, and Schwaegler's reference to a mysterious Professor Kronstetter.

The clue to Kronstetter was discovered, accidentally of course, by the bumbling hotel owner, who had found a yellowing newspaper article about Kronstetter lining the bottom of a cutlery tray. The photograph of Kronstetter showed a suitably attired Rommel who had presumably buried arms, fuel and water in the Egyptian desert before the war—a clear fiction since German troops were only sent to North Africa on the spur of the moment—but a clever plot device that also served to solace bruised Allied egos.

Told by the Field Marshal that he will soon be dispatched through the British lines to Alexandria to pave the way for Rommel's triumphal entrance, Bramble has only a few hours to discover the location of Kronstetter's graves. The five graves remain a mystery, until he looks in a gazetteer and discovers that the only letters cited by Schwaegler in his reports to Rommel had to be the printed *Egypt* on the Field Marshal's map. An Allied air attack provides both the excuse for Bramble to copy the map and for the only real fight in the film, since an Allied near-miss partially uncovers the body of the real Davos, a sight that is not missed by Schwaegler. Bramble survives the fight with the lieutenant, but is almost betrayed by Mouche, who had been counting on the young officer to help her brother. Schwaegler had told her that for some favors a lieutenant was as good as a Field Marshal. About to tell the Germans about Bramble, Mouche is summoned by Rommel who is furious about his missing adjutant. Told by a scornful Rommel that all the telegrams concerning her brother had been faked by Schwaegler, she proudly insists that she has killed the lieutenant, when the guards finally find his body. Bramble is free to receive an official motorcycle escort through the British lines.

Even this climactic scene was stolen by Stroheim who was seen and heard cursing in German as Mouche descends the stairs. In a sequence that must have amused the refugee writers, Wilder and Biro, as well as Stroheim, Rommel was heard asking his men angrily whether this was the German Army or a Jews' school and then to comment on Schwaegler's sexual affair with the Frenchwoman. These lines were soon followed by a dialogue reference to Stroheim's role as Rauffenstein in *The Grand Illusion,* since he told Mouche that her trial would not be conducted according to German law, but "to show you we are not the barbarians you think—according to your own law, the Code Napoleon."

The success of Bramble's impromptu espionage mission was shown by means of ani-

A quick-witted O'Connell (center, Richard Conte) dissuades factory detective from arresting O'Connell's colleague Lassiter (right, Frank Latimore). *(13 Rue Madeleine)*

mated maps and newsreel clips of the British victory at El Alamein. Although fanciful propaganda as far as the actual secret of the five graves was concerned, Wilder's film did tackle some of the war's serious themes. There was the detailed, if stylized, characterization of the two Germans; the ambivalence surrounding Italian participation in the war as exemplified by a bumbling but humane Italian general, and the possibility of French collaboration as shown by Mouche. Of course, neither Wilder nor Brackett nor Biro asked the hard question whether she would have saved Bramble if Schwaegler hadn't been such a cad. There was also the apparent ease with which Bramble carried off his impersonation, especially since Schwaegler had boasted of the Teutonic unwillingness even to enter a darkened room without knowing the location of the light switch. Despite Mouche's off-screen execution at the hands of the Germans, *Five Graves to Cairo* verged on the humorous, possibly because of Tone's performance as the ironical innocent cast into the role of a double-agent. He made jokes with Mouche about not being a gallant German officer and traded anti-German comments with the despised Italian gen-

eral, and as played against Stroheim's overly histrionic Rommel and Van Eyck's sleek lieutenant, Bramble emerged the representative of British reserve and understatement.

Wilder's film was, of course, a wartime production and its producer, Charles Brackett, seeing it years later reported that it left him with "the dreadful smell of propaganda." Spy films set in the wartime period, however, were naturally open to this charge, but one film which required severe editing to align it with official policy was Fritz Lang's *Cloak and Dagger*. This 1946 production not only had the directorial skills of one of the film world's founding masters, but also the cooperation of several advisers experienced in the "cloak and dagger" operations of the Office of Strategic Services, the wartime predecessor to the CIA. That cooperation turned into governmental interference, since Lang's film treatment called for the mention of uranium in its story of atomic bomb research and the government insisted on the use of the less precise synonym, pitchblende.

The word pitchblende in the report of an Allied agent began the film as written by Ring Lardner, Jr., and Albert Maltz. As interpreted

Suzanne (Annabella) prepares to jump into occupied Europe along with double agent O'Connell (right, Richard Conte) and Lassiter (Frank Latimore), as flight sergeant (Karl Malden) looks on. *(13 Rue Madeleine)*

Spy trainer Bob Sharkey (James Cagney) and Suzanne (Annabella) radio in an Allied pick-up plane. *(13 Rue Madeleine)*

by OSS officials, the only way to discover how far German research had progressed was to send a scientist to Europe for firsthand observation. That physicist was soon found, a tweed-suited Alvah Jasper (Gary Cooper), conducting experiments in his university laboratory. Asked to undertake the assignment by an old school friend, Jasper responds, "There was a time when I thought I wanted to be some kind of secret agent—I gave it up when I was eight." The mission he accepted appeared deceptively simple, merely to interview a famous Hungarian scientist being protected by the Americans in Switzerland, the land where spies bloom during every war. Jasper accepts grudgingly; he complains of all the scientific talent and money being expended on a bomb, but he soon sees the crimes of which the enemy is capable, even in neutral Switzerland. The Hungarian physicist, Katherine Loder (Helene Thimig), is distraught over the consequences of her defection upon hostages in her homeland. Jasper must not only prevent her return but also find out information, but he has inadvertently signed her death warrant upon his arrival in Switzerland. By scrupulously avoiding an airport photographer Jasper has given notice to German agents that he is more than a mere importer of wristwatches. As a result Loder is kidnapped and killed by German spies who have been traced and surrounded by American agents, including Jas-

per. The only resort left is for the American physicist to convince another key researcher, the Italian Dr. Polda, into defecting, but for this effort Jasper must enter an Italy teeming with Fascist militia and Nazi troops. This shift to Italy not only heightened the suspense, since the chances of capture and the risks of execution were far greater than in Switzerland, but also supplied romantic interest in the person of a Resistance fighter, Gina (Lilli Palmer).

A hardened veteran who is initially seen knifing a German sentry, Gina is frankly contemptuous of Jasper. After all, he is neither a European (his name today seems a conscious parody of WASP America), nor a seasoned anti-fascist, nor an experienced secret operative, and she notes that he doesn't look the part of a German scientist, a role he would have to play in order to see Polda. Actually, Gary Cooper did seem out of his depth in the role of a scientist turned spy, and even with trilby, wing collar, accent and monocle, he didn't look like a German scientist, although the script thankfully had him fooling an Italian secret policeman and not a German one. Although the fascist counter-measures were never shown on screen, a notable deviation from *Spies* and Lang's own preference for showing both sides of an intrigue, the enemy in *Cloak and Dagger* was given a great deal of credit for cunning.

Despite Gina's fears and the viewers' possible disbelief, Jasper does get to see Polda (Vladimir Sokoloff) and learns that Polda's co-operation had been obtained by holding his daughter as a hostage. Jasper promises to free her, but this meeting too is betrayed by a small oversight—the kind that matters in espionage. To get rid of the Italian security agent, Polda asks him to fetch a box of matches, but upon his return, while Jasper and Polda bade each other farewell in German, the plainclothesman notices a full matchbox already on Polda's desk—a subtle and realistic hint from the maker of *Spies*.

Realism even suffuses the love scenes between Gina and Jasper. She finds a safe hideout for them in the apartment of a woman friend, a Fascist whose mantelpiece is decked with framed autographed photos of her lovers, all of them German officers, while in an earlier hideout Jasper has amused himself in her absence by doodling algebraic formulae on the walls. As American as Jasper was in the interpretation by Cooper, this was his appeal for Gina, since he represented a people and nation untouched by warring ideologies and governments. Their budding romance, however, took second place to the film's plot which soon had the pair of them dodging the security man who had apparently followed Jasper since his visit with Polda. Jasper's fight with the man was a good suspense sequence, since Jasper, a relatively inexperienced agent must not only kill his opponent, but do so without attracting the attention of any of the people passing through the hallway into which Gina had lured him. The apparent success of the plan to release Polda's daughter and fly them, along with Jasper, out of Italy soon sours when the daughter proudly admits in front of the incredulous Polda that she is a German impersonator and that his real daughter has been taken to Germany and shot weeks ago. She then declares that they are surrounded by German troops and had better surrender. Without a moment's hesitation, Gina guns her down and the traditional shoot-out between beleaguered Allied agents and advancing German troops begins. The major suspense concerned Polda and Jasper's dash for the waiting Allied plane, while a secondary concern was whether Gina would choose to fly out with Jasper. Gina naturally chooses to remain behind —a role played with increasing depth by Palmer in a number of spy films.

Palmer, herself a refugee from Nazi Germany, was able to impart to her roles both the sexual appeal of an attractive woman and the efficiency of a dedicated spy who can both kill and be killed without regret. In a recent, mediocre film, *Operation Crossbow,* she cold-bloodedly murdered a Sophia Loren who had inadvertently discovered that an Allied spy was using her dead husband's identity in a plan to sabotage German rocket production. Like Lukas, Veidt and Peter Lorre, Palmer was one of the Nazi legacies to the Anglo-American film industry.

Pressures to change the film's script did not end with the substitution of pitchblende for uranium, but resulted in a significant alteration as well. Jasper's faint opposition to atomic bomb research at the film's opening still exists in most prints, but according to a recent interview with Albert Maltz just published by Barbara Zheutlin and David Talbot, an entire reel, one whole episode, was cut from the film by Warners above Lang's objections. That episode detailed Jasper's search in Germany for traces of Nazi atomic secrets and had one of its characters exclaim, "It's Year One of the Atomic Age and God have mercy on us all," to which the physicist responded:

> No, no, God have mercy on us only if we're fools. God have mercy on us if we ever thought we could really keep science a secret or ever wanted to. God have mercy on us if we think we can wage other wars without destroying ourselves, and God have mercy on us if we haven't the sense to keep the world at peace.*

Lieutenant Commander Ewen Montagu (Clifton Webb) gets the official go-ahead for Operation Mincemeat, while his secretary, Pam (Josephine Griffin), looks on. *(The Man Who Never Was)*

*Creative Differences, Boston: South End Press, 1978, p. 37.

Major William Martin about to be launched on his mission, while production crew and extras man the conning tower. *(The Man Who Never Was)*

Preparing the body of Major William Martin, Royal Marines, seems an easier task for Montagu (Clifton Webb) than for his aide, George Acres (Robert Flemyng). *(The Man Who Never Was)*

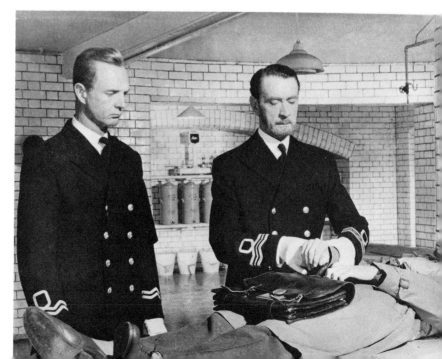

In very dramatic terms *Cloak and Dagger* depicted the reluctance with which many Anglo-American and refugee scientists approached the task of making the atomic bomb, and the force used by the Nazis to compel such work in many of their researchers. By filtering such a message into his war period spy film, Lang, in conjunction with Maltz and Lardner, had touched upon one of the raw nerves soon to bring on the collapse of the wartime Grand Alliance and to begin the Cold War. Few film writers and directors were willing to be so bold in the fifties.

Many were content to reevaluate the older espionage war with renewed emphasis on details and complex intrigues. Henry Hathaway and Louis de Rochemont, whose collaboration had resulted in *The House on 92nd Street,* created one more anti-Nazi spy film, again with an address as its title, *13 Rue Madeleine.* Also characteristic of their work was the film's opening scenes, the National Archive in Washington, D.C., from whose files the film's story was supposedly drawn and not from the imagination of screen writers John Monks, Jr., and Sy Bartlett. Indeed, the film's fictional second half has been unfavorably compared with its quasi-documentary first half. Following the training of three agents for Operations 77 (because of a dispute with OSS

German agent O'Reilly (Stephen Boyd) asking about his late, lamented friend Major William Martin. *(The Man Who Never Was)*

Chief Donovan, the name of that organization was disallowed in the film), the film had two stories, the mission to capture a French collaborationist engineer and the discovery of a German agent among the three volunteers. O'Connell, Lassiter and Suzanne (Richard Conte, Frank Latimer and Annabella), were seen resting in the Virginian country house requisitioned by Operations 77, while their instructor-chief, Robert Sharkey (James Cagney), must decide which of his students is a trained Abwehr agent named Kuncel.

The training exercises are shown in de-

The discovery of the body on the Iberian coast. *(The Man Who Never Was)*

Pam's roommate, Lucy (Gloria Grahame), whose sorrow over the death of her lover helps assure O'Reilly of the major's identity. *(The Man Who Never Was)*

tail, from memorization of the events in a short newsclip through cross-country hikes to simulated interrogations and, of course, the standard training, radio telegraphy. O'Connell and Lassiter are becoming close friends and are assigned together to complete a graduation exercise—the infiltration of an actual defense plant to get a photograph of a torpedo detonator. The pair are the only students to succeed, largely because of O'Connell's provident use of a falsified security clearance card and his willingness to accuse Lassiter of being a spy in front of the local watchman. The top student of his class, O'-Connell, is seen by Sharkey as the only possible suspect for the role of Kuncel. To detour Kuncel, Sharkey assigns him special duties concerning an Allied invasion through Holland. A feint, the idea was to give Kuncel false information and then to allow him to jump into Europe with Lassiter and Suzanne where he would certainly join his own side. Sharkey tells Lassiter the complete story, since if Kuncel does not disappear once in Europe, Lassiter must kill him. Lassiter is Sharkey's insurance policy, if the plan to deceive Kuncel fails. On board the plane, however, Kuncel is quick to notice the abrupt change in the normally friendly Lassiter. As they prepare to bail out, Kuncel deftly cuts Lassiter's rip cord. Not only has the great deception failed, but Kuncel is now in a position to trap all the Operation 77 agents.

In a melodramatic decision, heightened unfortunately by Cagney's performance, Sharkey jumps into France, both to locate the collaborator and to deny Kuncel his success. With the help of a local Resistance leader (Sam Jaffe), Sharkey does capture the engineer, but in the course of the operation is caught himself by a Kuncel now wearing his Wehrmacht officer's uniform.

Kuncel was perhaps the most interesting character in the film. A seasoned professional whose conduct echoed Sharkey's earlier admonition that war was no game and that no agent was a good sport, Kuncel not only cold-bloodedly killed Lassiter, he also showed no hesitation in pulling a fellow German officer into Sharkey's line of fire in order to save himself. He also paced nervously in front of the door behind which he knew Sharkey was being tortured by Gestapo men, and nearly orders an end to the torture. The film's emphasis on both sides' efficiency did approach the imaginary, however. The German radio-direction finding vans, the Gestapo and Kuncel displayed a teamwork that was unthinkable to any series of bureaucracies, let alone the Nazi one, while the Maquis obeyed Sharkey's instructions with a devotion that would have astounded De Gaulle. This departure from reality marked the film's climax, when a squadron of low-flying bombers are assigned the task of destroying the building at 13 Rue Madeleine, the Gestapo headquarters where Sharkey is being interrogated.

Despite its lapses, Hathaway's and de Rochemont's film did point the way for future spy films set in the wartime period: realistic details, on-location shooting, formidable opponents and plausible stories and plots. At times directors and screen writers chose to fashion their films almost totally on espionage feats that had recently been made public. Ronald Neame and Nigel Balchin chose this path for their 1956 production, *The Man Who Never Was*.

Based on the non-fiction book by a former intelligence officer, Ewen Montagu, the film depicted an actual Allied exercise in what would soon be called disinformation—deliberate rumormongering to give an enemy false clues as to your real intentions. To disguise the plan to invade Sicily, the British invented a marine major, a corpse carrying military papers whose body washed onto the Iberian coast would be spotted by German agents and whose documents would hint strongly at an Allied invasion of Greece. The central problem for Royal Navy Commander Montagu (Clifton Webb) was obtaining a corpse of the right age who had died of water accumulation in the lungs. As his assistant, George Acres (Robert Flemying), commented, "Every body belongs to somebody." The letters crucial to the plan, personal letters from one Allied general to another, were relatively easy to get, particularly since Webb's Commander Montagu seemed to intimidate his aides, Ministerial superiors, generals and most viewers alike.

A body was eventually found, and the film's best moment was the meeting between Montagu and the father (Moultree Kelsall), who must be persuaded into donating his son's body for a use about which he can know nothing. The other virtue in the film was the detail with which a false identity, Major William Martin, must be created. Bank accounts, club memberships (an English officer must be a member of some clubs), theater ticket stubs, loose change and a love letter had to be supplied. The love letter was dictated by a secondary character, Lucy (Gloria Grahame), whose own love life provided a convenient mirror to

Eric Erickson (William Holden) records details of his mission while British control, Collins (right, Hugh Griffith), listens. *(The Counterfeit Traitor)*

the imaginary major. On the night of the operation, code-named Mincemeat, while a British submarine buries the major at sea, Montagu and his secretary watch a comedy that reduced the audience to hysterics, but leave the pair unaffected—their thoughts are on the tidal patterns off the Portugese coast. The audience soon saw that coastline and the villagers who brought the body and its manacled briefcase to the British Consular officials, but not without attracting the attention of two men watching from the balcony of the German Consulate.

Montagu and his staff are then faced with

At gala reception in Berlin, Eric Erickson (William Holden) meets Nazi leaders. *(The Counterfeit Traitor)*

Marianne Mollendorf (right, Lilli Palmer) adjusts Erickson's (William Holden) handkerchief as recognition signal at Berlin Reception. *(The Counterfeit Traitor)*

the problem that the operation may have miscarried, if the Germans haven't photographed the false letters. Scientific investigations by a characteristically fussy researcher (Miles Malleson) reveal that the letters have indeed been pressed flat, photographed and refolded. There is only one more final proof of German credulity, the arrival of an agent to confirm Major Martin's identity. That agent soon arrives in the guise of an Irish salesman, O'Reilly (Stephen Boyd). Ironically, the most conventional segment of the film revolves around O'Reilly, since he is the one who must proceed with caution while finding out about the Major and must transmit his findings to Berlin where Abwehr head, Admiral Canaris, waits. Smiling broadly, with as thick a brogue to match, O'Reilly begins to ask the assistant bank manager, whom Montagu had warned about possible queries, about his old friend,

Major Martin. Now the originator of Operation Mincemeat knows the Germans have swallowed the bait and are about to digest it whole. While O'Reilly is busily stringing up his antenna across the dingy boarding house room and then transmitting his report to Berlin with the mandatory Luger at his side on the bed, the British counter-intelligence are rushing to arrest him, until Montagu realizes that his arrest would signal the Abwehr that Major Martin had indeed been a fake, the creation of British Intelligence who had captured the agent sent to investigate him. After all, what was one more dead British officer to the spy masters, unless they had created him? O'Reilly was allowed to complete his mission and leave, and as a result German units were withdrawn from Sicily.

The Man Who Never Was unfortunately had a very undramatic quality, since much of the action revolved around a dead body seen only in glimpses. Webb's performance was too restrained and cold, while Grahame as the American librarian with the RAF lover whose death O'Reilly confused with Martin's was perhaps too maudlin. More could have been made of O'Reilly and the enemy efforts to decipher the misinformation, and one crucial question was never asked in a film that stressed the peculiar details of spycraft—every German unit transferred from Sicily did mean an easier invasion, but also meant that those same divisions would be able to fight another time and perhaps to greater advantage elsewhere. Ronald Neame's film was too closely bonded to the banal routine of professional

Polish worker (Emil Stetzer) hanged by SS troops as warning to other refinery workers. *(The Counterfeit Traitor)*

Marianne Mollendorf (Lilli Palmer) has just discovered she has given her confession, not to a priest, but to a Gestapo agent. *(The Counterfeit Traitor)*

espionage without enough dramatic tone. Another postwar memoir lent itself to a sounder cinematic treatment: Alexander Klein's *The Counterfeit Traitor* was skillfully transferred to the screen by George Seaton, who both directed and wrote the screenplay for Paramount in 1961.

Born in Brooklyn, Eric Erickson (William Holden) is a naturalized Swedish businessman neutral enough to deal with both the Germans

147

and Allies, until he discovers his name on a published list of Nazi sympathizers. Shocked and angry, he soon discovers that his inclusion on that list is a device to force him to work for British Intelligence whose representative, Collins (Hugh Griffith), he meets on the sly at a Stockholm hotel. Collins not only admits the blackmail, but compounds it by having the conversation taped to enforce Erickson's cooperation, since the Swedes strongly value their neutrality. Disarmed as well as astounded by Collins' cynicism, Erickson has to agree to become a spy, while the spy master, between courses of his luncheon, admits he would use a drug addict or a sexual pervert to help his nation. Not only must Erickson supply information on the German oil industry, he has to act the part of someone on the Allied blacklist. Despite his real sympathies, Erickson must make spiteful remarks about the Allies, and more importantly, has to drop sneering remarks about Jews and to insult publicly a Jewish friend within hearing of the German ambassador. Although suspected by the embassy's SS liaison, soon both the unwilling spy and the Reich's diplomat are sharing polite jokes over the SS man's transfer to occupied Copenhagen where, the ambassador remarks, he can strut around again in uniform.

The friendship with the ambassador is needed to secure official sanction for Erickson's plan to construct German oil refineries in Sweden—the means by which he is to secure the information the Allies want. Erickson not only humors the German, he also promises him a share in the company he is forming and charmingly pays him the money lost in weekly bridge games. The efficacy of the Swede's behavior as plotted by Collins soon bears fruit, when the German accidentally discovers Erickson's espionage role and threatens to tell both Berlin and Stockholm. Erickson calmly shows him the cancelled checks made payable to the ambassador, clear proof that he also was implicated in espionage. Leaving the bewildered ambassador, Erickson asks, "Did you really think I was such a poor bridge player?"

Erickson begins his frequent business trips to Germany with a gala reception during which he makes contact with another agent, a woman with whom he is to pretend to have an affair, Marianne (Lilli Palmer). The wife of a high-ranking German officer, Marianne is both an idealist and an efficient spy. She would embrace and kiss Erickson for the sake of any Gestapo man trailing them and then primly shake hands before getting down to the business of encoding messages. Her shock at Erickson's selfish reasons for being a spy contrasted with her own, a staunch belief in the Catholic obligation to fight the antichrist, Hitler. In perhaps the film's most moving scene, she tells him that one must not think of the

Erickson (William Holden) is brought to Berlin's SS headquarters for questioning. *(The Counterfeit Traitor)*

war simply in terms of tanks and planes, but in terms of a truck on its way to a concentration camp and what is shivering inside that truck.

Unlike many other spy films set during the war, *The Counterfeit Traitor* stressed the personal and emotional cost of espionage: Eric Erickson had not only to forsake his wife and friends, who were upset by his apparent Nazi sympathies, he had also to witness Nazi atrocities first-hand. During a visit to an oil refinery he sees the cold-blooded execution of a Polish slave laborer chosen at random from among a group of protesting workers. This revelation thrusts him closer to Marianne's idealism, but she too is tormented by her work. The Allied bombs she helped direct at oil refineries often took the lives of innocent civilians as well. To assuage this guilt she drags Erickson off to a nearby cathedral to help tend the wounded, and then the following morning while comforting each other they hear the dreaded and familiar sound, the squeal of tires in the street and the rush of footfalls on the staircase. The boots miraculously pass their door, however, and can be heard above them where a man with anti-Nazi leaflets is beaten and arrested. So a friend unknown to them has been arrested and taken away, but they are safe for the moment.

Marianne's faith ironically ends their safety, since she attends church followed by two Gestapo men, one of whom detains the local cleric, while the other takes Marianne's confession about her role in the recent bombing raid. Erickson realizes the danger only when, upon his last business trip to Germany to retrieve incriminating evidence from a dead friend's files, he is whisked away from the airport by an SS man with the black-and-white SD diamond of the Security Service on his sleeve. Driven to Berlin's central headquarters for Reich security, Erickson sees the Nazis' victims waiting terrified in hallways near nondescript office doors, while uniformed officers and secretaries flirt in stair-

Having witnessed Marianne's execution in the yard of Moabit Prison, Erickson (William Holden) must endure SS Colonel Nordorff's (Wolfgang Preiss) patient probe for information. (*The Counterfeit Traitor*)

wells. Taken to a Berlin prison, Erickson has a view of the courtyard where several ragged women prisoners including Marianne are machine-gunned.

Despite his grief, Erickson has enough cool nerve to realize that the two high-ranking SS officers who appeared shortly after Marianne's execution were fishing for information, that had they known of his role in her espionage he would have been dealt with as summarily. On their part the SS men are divided over the need for security, their suspicions about Erickson and the administrative turmoil of arresting a neutral businessman without formal charges and evidence. The Nazi compromise is to have Erickson followed assiduously by an experienced Gestapo man, Jaeger

Erickson (William Holden) slugs Gestapo man Jaeger (Stefan Schnabel). (*The Counterfeit Traitor*)

(Stefan Schnabel), who follows Erickson to the funeral of his friend. There Jaeger appeals to the dead man's son, Hans (Helo Gutschwager), an inquisitive Hitler Youth, as "one soldier to another." Hans had learned of his father's espionage and Erickson's role in it, but the clever Swede had warned the boy that the Nazis would never permit him to remain a member of the *Hitler Jugend* once they learned of his father's treachery. Erickson's nerve and brains are prepared even for the confrontation with Jaeger; he not only kills the Gestapo man with his own gun, but takes his identity disk to avoid arrest by the policemen drawn to the scene by the shot. Eventually Erickson makes his way to Copenhagen, where friendly fishermen who have been ferrying Jews to Sweden take him and a sickly Jewish refugee to safety. The German naval patrol which stops them does nothing; the inspecting officer sees the coat with the worn patch in the shape of a Jewish star and lets the matter drop. Erickson arrives back in Sweden, but the Jew (Klaus Kinsky) has suffocated himself rather than give away their hiding place by coughing.

Unlike many other films of its type, *The Counterfeit Traitor* was sobering to a remarkable degree. Erickson, the spy-against-his-will, has not only lost his wife and stable life in Sweden, but also his lover in Germany, Marianne. He has seen several people die as a result of the Nazis, besides her, and is met at the Swedish entry point by the distant, professional praise of Collins, his control. The only happy ending in this film was the fact that his Jewish friend, Max (Ulf Palme), was there to greet him on his walk from the dreary ferry landing.

The lost romance in this film was a grim departure from the traditionally glamorous love lives of the cinematic spy. Romance, after all, had been one of the profession's benefits, and although romance and love existed in the more modern spy dramas, it was often part of the spy masters' scheme as in *The Spy Who Came in from the Cold,* or a corollary to the hero's trial by ordeal as in *The 39 Steps* and *Three Days of the Condor.* There was a time, however, when erotic romance was the prime motive of the spy film, not any dull political message or technical secret. In an era of Victorian double standards and Puritan repression, the female spy was allowed the sexual license granted only Don Juan and Casanova, and even today the touch of romance still lingers in the modern spy film.

Hitler Youth member Hans Holtz (Helo Gutschwager) steals Erickson's (William Holden) briefcase containing incriminating letter. (*The Counterfeit Traitor*)

6

The Touch of Romance

The Great Love
Dishonored
Mata Hari
Secret Agent
Night Train to Munich
Casablanca
Notorious
The Golden Earrings

Adventure and politics, loyalty and war were not the only important elements in the spy film. Espionage may have been looked upon as dangerous and illicit, but it was also seen as mysterious and exciting. Spying had been infused with the aura of the romantic as thickly as any gothic novel. In the silent serials the plight of the trapped, endangered hero(ine) was often linked to a love story. This symbiosis between espionage and romance was already established in the popular mind when D. W. Griffith gave it cinematic form in *The Great Love*. In this 1918 production, an English girl whose sweetheart was fighting the Germans in France found herself courted by a man who turned out to be a German agent. This theme of double betrayal, the individual as well as the national, was to appear in many forms in later films. The tale of romance often eclipsed the espionage theme, which provided the background and plot devices for the personal story. Romance was, after all, a human impulse likely to endanger a spy, but was found more interesting by audiences than the details of spycraft. The unfaithful lover and the en-

emy agent were often one and the same character, and for nearly a decade the world's most famous spy remained a woman, Mata Hari.

A product of actual history and the standards of Edwardian society, the myth of Mata Hari has outweighed and outlived the bare truth. Born in the Dutch East Indies, Margarita Gertrud Zelle was an exotic dancer who may have been a German agent betrayed by Berlin, or a double-agent who lost her footing in that fatal game, or an adventuress who dabbled thoughtlessly in espionage, or just a silly flirt who hadn't the faintest idea what she was doing. Despite the reality, Mata Hari was to become, and remain until James Bond, the popular embodiment of romance and espionage, sexuality and betrayal. The idea of the woman spy whose beauty allowed her to destroy an enemy had its roots in the Old Testament where both Judith and Delilah epitomized the moral and immoral spy, and even then, depending upon which side you were on. Marlene Dietrich and Greta Garbo, the two most popular actresses of their era, both played spies in productions that used the First

Despite the Austrian Uniform, Victor McLaglen is really Colonel Kranau, Russian agent H-14, while, despite her embrace, Marlene Dietrich is X-27. (Dishonored)

World War as the background to their eroti-cally tinged tales of espionage, *Dishonored* and *Mata Hari.*

Directed by Josef von Sternberg, from his own story idea, *Dishonored* told the story of an Austrian spy, X-27 (Marlene Dietrich), who managed to function superbly as an agent, but chose to die romantically as a woman. Made in 1931 for Paramount, the film first shows Die-trich as a Viennese streetwalker whose defiant retort to a policeman, "I'm not afraid of life or death," attracts the attention of a bystander, who turns out to be the chief of the Austrian Secret Service (Gustav von Seyffertitz). He ac-companies her to her apartment where he asks if she would be willing to spy against Aus-tria; her refusal and calling of a policeman assures him of her loyalty. The prostitute is made a secret agent: X-27. In her conversa-tions with the Viennese spy master she sits in an armchair, her fur-trimmed dress raised provocatively above her knee in the pose that was to become an important visual signature in the film. As a spy, her first assignment is to discover whether an Austrian officer, Colonel von Hindau (Warner Oland), has been pass-ing secrets to the Russians. Following a lavish costume ball where she flirts with the suspect colonel, the pair are riding back to his apart-ment when they offer a lift to one of the revel-ers dressed as a clown. In return, the clown offers Hindau a cigarette, while X-27 later learns from the colonel's valet that Hindau is a nonsmoker. She recognizes that the cigarette contained a message and calls the Secret Ser-vice. When Hindau realizes that his secret has been discovered, he shoots himself rather than face the disgrace of a court-martial and firing squad. This success leads to her next task, the discovery of the clown, Hindau's Rus-sian contact, known as H-14.

While posing as a Polish peasant girl in a village on the border, she has to avoid the am-orous attentions of a Russian officer (Lew Cody) in pursuit of the man she has identified as H-14, Colonel Kranau (Victor McLaglen). Kranau, however, has recognized her and she avoids capture by drugging his wine. Kranau has to follow her back toward the Austrian lines. Once on Austrian-held territory, she succeeds in capturing him, but the demands of romance were more important than espio-nage. X-27 purposefully toys with her revolv-er, dropping it so that Kranau can make his escape before the arrival of the Austrian po-lice. For this breach of security, X-27 has to face a firing squad.

The personal, romantic element triumph-

As X-27, Marlene Dietrich receives her orders from the Austrian Secret Service chief (Gustav Von Seyffertitz). *(Dishonored)*

ed in the sequence in which she died. Rather than dress in the leather trench coat, the uniform of the anonymous asexual spy, or the striped coat of a prisoner, she chooses to wear the lavish clothes of a streetwalker. As a final gesture of defiance, she languidly lights a cigarette and adjusts her garter, while the firing squad whose officer had initially refused to shoot a woman puts an end to the career of X-27.

Like its more famous successor *Mata Hari, Dishonored* played on the mixture of sexuality and efficiency surrounding the female spy. She had to be flirtatious, yet ruthless, alluring yet deadly, without becoming emotionally distant. X-27 had proved herself the equal of H-14. Not only had she eluded his attempt to capture her, but she also had caught him and then allowed him to escape in a gesture that was evidence of her basic femininity. Like Sonia in Lang's *Spies,* X-27 had chosen the demands of romance over the reasons of state and dressed accordingly at the film's conclusion. Any discussion of the message in Hindau's cigarette or the importance of capturing Kranau was totally extraneous to the depiction of the female spy as unequal mixtures of sinner and saint.

The height of this romantic notion, however, was, and shall probably remain, *Mata Hari,* George Fitzmaurice's 1932 film version of the legendary spy's story. The film's theme was more of betrayed love than traded military secrets, and like *Dishonored* the spycraft depicted served mainly as background to the featured performers. As a spy and dancer, Mata Hari (Greta Garbo) could be seen amid luxurious surroundings surrounded by admiring older statesmen and young officers. And isn't that what being a spy used to mean in the old days? As seen in Fitzmaurice's film, Mata Hari was less enigmatic than Sternberg's X-27. While the Austrian prostitute was depicted as a competent agent and a skilled dissembler who could act the perfect peasant girl, Garbo's Mata Hari never acted out of character. Her story was one of a true love, fated by the war and the German espionage system, to a tragic end. Her lover, a Russian pilot, Lieutenant Alexis Rosanoff (Ramon Novarro), was shot down and blinded, because of the information she had supplied her superiors. Although the film contained a hint of betrayal on the part of the Germans, the major theme was Mata Hari's remorse over the fate of her Russian pilot. The tearful conclusion had the famous spy carry out one more pretense: she made believe for his benefit that she was in a hospital facing death rather than in a military prison about to be stood against a wall. Her contrition and remorse also seemed to stem more from her series of infidelities rather than from any deed of espionage, most of which appeared pointless and farfetched. Since both women had worked for the wrong side, were in fact Delilahs, and not Judiths, their virtues lay in the stylized bravery with which they met their deaths, as well as the acts of selflessness connected with their espionage, particularly X-27's conscious mistake with her prisoner.

In both *Dishonored* and *Mata Hari*, the female spies were seen as professionals, conscious adversaries who knew what they were about and the risks they ran. Although tainted politically by the side for which they worked, the Mata Hari spy was still looked upon as a complicated character, neither the evil genius nor the sexy traitoress of Lang's *Spies*. Like the conscious male spy, however, the female agent also suffered a virtual eclipse as the decade reached its midpoint. She was soon replaced by a total innocent cast into the spy war, but

with a significant difference—while the male character tried to solve the mystery, the woman tended to remain incredulous, even hostile. Passive and resistant, the woman trailed after, or was dragged along by the male character in his pursuit of the elusive secret or the antagonistic spymaster. If this resembled the sexual stereotyping according to the Victorian standard, it was heightened by granting the woman an ancillary importance to the plot; she became the romantic reward at the film's conclusion. Even where the woman spy was an enemy, as in *The House on 92nd Street* or *The Iron Curtain,* she was never to be allowed the complexity of a Greta Garbo or Marlene Dietrich, nor even the total fanaticism of a Haghi.

The change from agent to love object was seen most clearly in a 1936 Alfred Hitchcock film, *Secret Agent.* Based on W. Somerset Maugham's *Ashenden,* the film told the story of two British spies and their colleague in search of a mysterious German agent operating out of Switzerland. Richard Ashenden (John Gielgud) is a novelist who has been transferred

A dazzlingly attired Mata Hari (Greta Garbo) receives instructions from her control, Andriani (Lewis Stone). *(Mata Hari)*

Mata Hari (Greta Garbo) knows that the young Lieutenant Rosanoff (Ramon Novarro) has already lost the game of espionage. *(Mata Hari)*

from the front to carry out an assignment in the neutral country with the aid of a fictitious wife, Elsa (Madeleine Carroll), and a professional assassin, the General (Peter Lorre). Elsa at one point cheerfully asks Ashenden whether there might be some gunplay, to which the battle-hardened officer grimaces his hope that there won't be any; in any case mur-

der was the General's department. The two men eventually find a clue and trace it to an Anglo-German couple living nearby, the Caypors (Florence Kahn and Percy Marmont). While Elsa takes a German lesson from Frau Caypor, Ashenden and the General go for a hike up a mountain with Herr Caypor. In a melodramatic flourish, the Caypors' pet

The Mexican general (left, Peter Lorre) reads a love note, while an incredulous Elsa Carrington (Madeleine Carroll) and a disapproving Richard Ashenden (John Gielgud) look on. *(Secret Agent)*

dachshund begins scratching at the door and howling the moment when the General pushes his master over the cliff's edge. Ashenden had been reluctant to kill the man in cold blood and is further stunned when he receives a coded message from London that Caypor was innocent and that the suspected German spy was leaving Switzerland shortly. Elsa, who has volunteered to become a spy, reacts to their error by leaving Switzerland with the American, Robert Marvin (Robert Young), who had been courting her since she had arrived at the hotel.

Initially whimsical and light-hearted, Marvin is somber and taciturn when Elsa approaches him, but he agrees to take her with

While Mata Hari (Greta Garbo) takes a chance on the turn of a card, the young Lieutenant Alexis Rosanoff standing over her shoulder (Ramon Novarro) will gamble with his life. *(Mata Hari)*

Karl Marsen (Paul Henreid) establishes contact with Anna Bomasch (Margaret Lockwood) in the concentration camp. *(Night Train to Munich)*

him to Turkey. Marvin, she soon discovers, is the German spy they had been assigned to track down and kill. Originally the hunters, Elsa, Ashenden and the General are themselves subject to arrest and execution, since Turkey is a German ally. The demand for a neat ending and the needs of the British Secret Service were combined in a convenient train wreck which fatally wounds Marvin, and a dying Marvin, in turn, shoots the General.

The film ended with a decided emphasis on pacifism and romance. At the conclusion of the war, the spy master who had recruited Ashenden receives a note from the former novelist and Elsa to the effect that they would never do espionage work again. "Peace at Last and the Last time," was the inter-title on the screen while the two lovers smiled at the audi-

ence. The change in Elşa from a would-be Mata Hari who could not adjust to the murderous reality of her fantasy was a far cry from Marlene Dietrich's acceptance of the bloodshed hidden behind most wartime espionage. Ashenden, too, was unwilling to face the grim reality, but he hadn't asked to be a spy, and had, after all, been transferred from the straightforward shooting war, so that his reluctance had the sanctity of gentlemanly honor.

If the woman could no longer be the prime protagonist in a spy film, she could be the object, like the military secret, of a duel between the rival male spies. This was the feature apparent in Carol Reed's 1940 film *Night Train to Munich.* Set in a Europe still at peace, this film, scripted by two of the genre's unher-

Anna Bomasch (Margaret Lockwood) meets music-hall performer and spy Gus Bennett (Rex Harrison). *(Night Train to Munich)*

A romantically inclined Karl Marsen (Paul Henreid) and a less-so Anna Bomasch (Margaret Lockwood). *(Night Train to Munich)*

alded creators, Sydney Gilliat and Frank Launder, combined several elements: a traditional spy story, a comment on life in Nazi Germany, the clash of German and English sensibilities and a classic love triangle decked out in patriotic colors. Produced for 20th Century-Fox by Edward Black, *Night Train to Munich* (sometimes re-titled *Night Train* for television broadcast) had more humor than any other wartime spy film, except for the outright comedies. Its opening, however, was a clever reminder of the years before the outbreak of hostilities. Starting with a very long-distance shot of an Alpine region, the camera closed in very slowly on a long, low mansion, then a section of wall, and finally a picture window through which men in uniform could be seen standing at attention before a solitary, screaming figure. Hitler was addressing his assembled generals, and soon a fist was seen, presumably the Führer's, smashing at a map labelled *Czechoslovakia.* The next sequence was newsreel footage of the German entry into Prague.

In the conquered city, the story centered on Axel Bomasch (James Harcourt) and his daughter Anna (Margaret Lockwood). An armor plate specialist, Bomasch is able to escape to England, but his daughter is seized by the Nazis and sent to a concentration camp where she meets fellow prisoner Karl Marsen (Paul Henreid). Together they plan an escape and

A suitably attired Gus Bennett (left, Rex Harrison) kisses the hand of Fraulein Bomasch (Margaret Lockwood), while her father (James Harcourt) looks on. *(Night Train to Munich)*

British Secret Service, as well as a rival for Anna's affections. Although owing her life to Karl, Anna is attracted by Gus's whimsical character, a vaudevillian variant of Sir Percy Blakeney, and soon realizes that Karl's real interest lies elsewhere. Anna and her father soon find themselves aboard a U-boat on whose conning tower stands Karl Marsen in the black uniform of a Gestapo agent. Gus Bennett must enter Germany to save both the armor specialist and his lovely daughter.

Part of the film's appeal and approach was to stress the efficacy of British intelligence (even a cinematic victory was welcome in 1940) and the tensions within the enemy's camp. Dressed in the full-dress uniform of a Wehrmacht major, complete to sword and monocle, Gus Bennett entered the Berlin office of the Reich's Naval Ministry. A pair of colleagues disguised as telephone repair men ensured that the appropriate call was made to welcome the bogus major. At the main hallway, however, Bennett sees that a pair of Gestapo men are assiduously requesting and checking "all identity cards, please, all identity cards." It was at this point that Gilliat and Launder melded their humor to a plot device. An altogether English-looking clerk, with black suit, bowler and umbrella, is slow in displaying his identity card and is set upon by the

eventually reach England. To rejoin her father, Anna Bomasch has to contact a seaside music-hall performer, Gus Bennett (Rex Harrison). Bennett is, of course, an agent of the

Gus Bennett (left, Rex Harrison) receiving his instructions from a classic grouping of intelligence and military chiefs. *(Night Train to Munich)*

Those eminently characteristic Caldicott and Charters (Naunton Wayne and Basil Radford, left) are not too distressed by the pair of new Germans. *(Night Train to Munich)*

two Gestapo guards, who have thick German accents.

"This is a fine country to line in," the little man mutters sarcastically under his breath, so that he becomes the prime target for the guards' concern. Faced by the Gestapo men whose fists rest belligerently on their hips, the clerk repeats his phrase with a smile replacing the sarcastic nuance. During this exchange, Bennett has carefully passed through the gate and stands behind them, so that he can immediately praise "the fine men of the Gestapo" for their vigilance. The two Nazi thugs snap to

attention and beam in appreciation. Bennett has now only to work his way up the hierarchy of a German military ministry to find the official who knows the whereabouts of the Bomasches.

Inside the ministry building, the script pursued two related themes: Bennett's noblesse oblige as a major and the clerk's uncharitable reference to Germany. The Gestapo men had dutifully reported the man's remark to his superior in the ministry, so that Bennett's question about Axel Bomasch and the dual interpretation of the clerk's comment

Trying to interpret Bennett's bogus credentials are (left to right): Schwab (Eliot Makeham); Kampenfeldt (Raymond Huntley); Admiral Hassiger (C.V. France); and controller (Kenneth Kent). *(Night Train to Munich)*

162

Gus Bennett (left, Rex Harrison) introduces himself to Charters and Caldicott (Basil Radford and Naunton Wayne) as a British spy. *(Night Train to Munich)*

went from one official to the next higher one. The ministry personnel were drawn from English characters, not Germans, and the prevalence of English accents was noticeable, even the clerk had been granted a British, rather than German, accent. The importance of aristocratic lineage was one of the film's jokes about the Germans, since all the higher-ranking naval officers and officials had portraits of the Kaiser or Hindenburg on their desks, not Hitler's. The Nazi bureaucrats, often depicted as semi-competent bourgeois, did not fail to mention this omission to their superiors who were often seen as passive, worldly wise noblemen from the Imperial period. Bennett uses this implied freemasonry of nobles when questioned about a relative, a man in the Foreign Ministry doing diplomatic work in the Balkans. Fearing a possible trap and deciding to attack his questioner, Bennett screws his monocle into place and responds

coldly, "And who is not doing diplomatic work in the Balkans?"

By such haughty means and the clever exploitation of the natural rivalry between Nazi upstarts and traditional Prussian officials, Bennett is able to locate Anna Bomasch and her father. The film, however, was not only a clash between British and German spies, since Bennett liked Anna and there was more than a hint that so did Karl. His pursuit of the fleeing trio was more than a matter of his job as their Gestapo guardian. That pursuit had as one of its sequences the inevitable train journey that was a realistic staple of pre-1945 Europe, the last peacetime train from Munich to the Swiss border. On board the same train with Bennett, still disguised as a Wehrmacht major, and the Bomasches, were those stereotypical officials from the British Foreign Ministry, Caldicott and Charters (Naunton Wayne and Basil Radford). The pair were struggling through their interpretation of political events and a grotesquely large edition of Hitler's *Mein Kampf*. Near the Swiss border, the chase boiled down to a gun duel between Bennett atop the cable car taking them to Switzerland and the Gestapo men led by Marsen. Wounded in the leg, Bennett's rival takes careful aim at the exposed British spy, but whether because the cable car has passed the invisible boundary between Germany and

Gus Bennett (Rex Harrison) holds off the Gestapo, so Anna and her father can gain time to escape. *(Night Train to Munich)*

Switzerland, or whether he feels that the better man had won, the Gestapo man doesn't shoot, and lets his gun drop.

Made early in the war, 1940, *Night Train to Munich* did not show any of the hatred and bitterness that was to develop. As depicted in Reed's film, espionage was a romantic duel; there was little bloodshed or violence and an aura of ironic good humor in a film that has remained one of the classics of its type. Romance and espionage were to become ingredients in an American film that served not only as a metaphor for the American national character, but was to become symbolic of the popular fascination with movies, *Casablanca*.

As written by Julius and Philip Epstein and Howard Koch from the play, *Everybody Comes to Rick's,* the 1943 Warner Brothers production was essentially another variant of the familiar theme of two men vying for the same woman's love. This love triangle in Michael Curtiz's film was set against a background of wartime intrigue and American isolationism. As Richard "Rick" Blaine, Humphrey Bogart played the part of the cafe owner whose cynical facade masked the soul of an embittered anti-fascist. Although he had fought in Spain and run guns to Ethiopia, Rick was a realist who fought the Nazis on his terms, not theirs. He may have denied gambling privileges to a German banker, but he also refuses to help the petty racketeer, Ugarte (Peter Lorre), cornered by the Vichy police. As a matter of fact, Rick seems to fit very comfortably into the refugee life in French Morocco. He chats as amiably with the Prefect of Police, Louis Renault (Claude Rains), as with the rival cafe owner, Ferarri (Sydney Greenstreet). The only person with whom he begins to clash is a recent arrival, the German plenipotentiary, Major Strasser (Conrad Veidt), but that conflict is eclipsed by another recent arrival to the seaport town, Ilsa Lund (Ingrid Bergman).

Ilsa's arrival is not accidental, nor that of Major Strasser; both are in Rick's Café Americain to retrieve "letters of transit signed by General De Gaulle"—letters that Ugarte had given Rick moments before his capture. Ilsa has also not arrived alone, but is accompanied by Victor Laszlo (Paul Henreid), a seasoned Resistance leader whose recent escape from a concentration camp and flight across Europe can be seen in a subtle two-inch scar over his right eye. Laszlo's character was not half as interesting as Rick's; the Resistance leader was a bloodless prig and as a result the actual political intrigue in *Casablanca* was easily eclipsed by Rick's relationship with Ilsa. Even the primary gimmick, the letters of transit, were im-

The creation of a cliché—the cable-car switch with British agent Gus Bennett (Rex Harrison) in the middle. *(Night Train to Munich)*

plausible; after all, when the film's action takes place, the fall of 1941, the Germans were winning the war they had started and General De Gaulle's name was not worth much in Vichy-controlled North Africa.

Torn between the ease of handing Laszlo over to Renault, and of course, Strasser, and using the letters of transit to leave Casablanca with Ilsa, Rick recounts his brief affair with her during the final days of unconquered Paris. Rick must choose between the personal and the abstract, between romance and the renewal of his political involvement. The other side of the triangle is far less certain. Although Ilsa was supposedly "the thing that kept him going", she not only tries to dissuade Laszlo from attending a local Resistance meeting, but she also displays an apparent amateur's interest in the war. Ilsa's role in the film was that of the traditional woman courted by two rivals, as well as a symbol of a beleaguered Europe.

The espionage motif was as transparent as the film's symbols; the openly opportunist Vichy police were accepted on a par with the pickpockets and refugees crowded into the port town. The only really evil characters were shown to be the German officers accompanying Major Strasser. Despite the implication of informers and spies, which was how Ugarte

Rick (left, Humphrey Bogart) can see what Victor (Paul Henreid) and Ilsa (Ingrid Bergman) cannot—that the film will have a happy ending. (*Casablanca*)

was caught, no fascist spies were seen in the film. Everyone, except Rick, wore his heart on his sleeve, and even Renault breezily told Strasser that he was indifferent to politics and merely blew with the wind. It was this linkage between distinct personalities and their symbolic role in occupied Europe that has earned *Casablanca* its millions of admirers. It was a singular tribute to the 1943 film audience that the screenplay needed no explication of the references to Ethiopia and Spain in Rick's past, while the duel of anthems, "Wacht am Rhein" and "La Marseillaise" could warm the hearts of any matinee crowd.

Although Ilsa was cast as the traditionally passive woman, this was not the sole role for an actress in a wartime spy film. Lilli Palmer as Gina in *Cloak and Dagger* or Bette Davis as Sara Muller in *Watch on the Rhine* played less traditional figures while remaining essentially feminine characters. In the 1967 film *La Guerre Est Finie*, Marianne (Ingrid Thulin) became an active, revolutionary spy in order to save her lover, Diego (Yves Montand). Of

Ugarte (right, Peter Lorre) is about to offer Rick (Humphrey Bogart) the letters of transit that will start a more lethal game of chess. (*Casablanca*)

course, Ingrid Bergman's persona differed widely from those of Bette Davis and Lilli Palmer, and it would be hard to envisage either of them asking, as does Bergman, that Humphrey Bogart do the thinking for both of them. There was also the implication at the close of *Casablanca* that Ilsa and Laszlo were leaving occupied Europe via neutral Lisbon for good. It was Rick and the recently converted Renault who went off to fight the fascists, an ending that rather baldly hinted at the European need to rely on its American ally.

With its victory of the politically moral over the romantically ambiguous, *Casablanca* fit a period in American life when all the studied mannerisms of Humphrey Bogart expressed a popular image of masculinity, and perhaps still does, when the cool menace of Major Strasser was enough for viewers unfamiliar with the real horrors of Nazi rule, and when people could still sense a better world beyond the newspaper accounts of the Allied landings in North Africa. By 1946 many of those feelings were gone, broken by a peace that seemed a prelude to another, far worse war. Espionage and politics were not suitable activities for featured characters, so that the careful balance of romance and espionage in Curtiz's film was not apparent in *Notorious*.

Written by Ben Hecht and directed by Alfred Hitchcock for RKO, *Notorious* was essentially a romance with a few indistinct spies added for suspense and motivation. Alicia Huberman (Ingrid Bergman) is seen as a thoroughgoing hedonist whose father, a Nazi sympathizer, is shown condemned by a Miami court in the film's opening sequence. At a house party following his conviction she meets a handsome party crasher, Devlin (Cary Grant), who turns out to be a government spy. Aware through recordings of her personal dislike of her father's politics, Devlin persuades her to undertake an espionage assignment in Rio de Janeiro. Her acceptance and her apparent reform (she has stopped heavy drinking) were part of the "very strange love affair," as she phrased it, that has grown between her and Devlin. Not only has she grown fond of him, she desperately wants him to believe in her, while Devlin remains distant, a somewhat apparent psychological defense. That reserve turns to ice when he learns the exact nature of her mission.

At a meeting with his superiors Devlin

At the airport in the fog, Rick Blaine (Humphrey Bogart) makes sure that Captain Louis Renault (Claude Rains) gives the proper orders for the safe passage of Ilsa and Victor Laszlo. (*Casablanca*)

learns that an old boyfriend of Alicia's, Alexander Sebastian (Claude Rains), is living nearby in great luxury, surrounded by a clique of Nazis and several German scientists. Alicia Huberman's job is to infiltrate that household to discover the purpose of their research. Devlin protests her possible unwillingness and her lack of training to carry out such an assignment, but his criticism is dismissed as a petty detail. When he leaves the briefing to see Alicia, Devlin also leaves behind a promised bottle of champagne, the symbol of his love for her. As the cynical, distant and professional agent Devlin cannot allow his feelings to complicate their assignment; he doesn't even admit to her that he has protested at the briefing on her behalf. Alicia Huberman renews her friendship with Sebastian with Devlin acting the role of an unlikely Cupid.

Sebastian was characterized more as a selfish and weak antagonist than a particularly evil one. Rather than a fanatical Nazi, Sebastian seemed an uprooted bon vivant forced to amuse himself in Brazil rather than in a Europe where "so many things have died for all of us." The only awesome character in the film was Madame Sebastian (Madame Konstantin), a Prussian grande dame who presided over the formal dinners in the Sebastian town house. At one of these dinners to which Alex-

At the dinner party, Alexander Sebastian (left, Claude Rains) must reassure Emil Hupke (Eberhard Krumschmidt), while another Nazi, Rossner (right, Peter Von Zerneck), looks on disapprovingly. *(Notorious)*

Devlin (left, Cary Grant) protests Alicia's assignment to his superior, Prescott (Louis Calhern), and another agent, Beardsley (Moroni Olsen). At far left is champagne bottle he'll forget. *(Notorious)*

167

The new Mrs. Sebastian (center, Ingrid Bergman) being shown her new home by servant, Joseph (Alex Minotis). *(Notorious)*

smugly dismisses her as "that sort of woman." It was a woman of "that sort," he counters, who was doing her patriotic duty as a spy in a dangerous assignment. Characteristically, Devlin does not say anything about this outburst to her, but continues to make snide references to her drinking and luxurious life as Mrs. Sebastian. Concurrent with this emotional suspense is the sequence involving the wedding party, during which Devlin and Alicia discover the champagne bottles full of a mysterious sand. Sebastian, the jealous and suspicious husband, has realized the real link between his bride and Devlin.

In a scene that is a splendid piece of understatement, Sebastian goes to his mother's ornate bedroom early in the morning to announce his discovery about Alicia. Madame Sebastian begins to gloat over his realization of her prediction, until she hears his revelation, "Mother, I'm married to an American agent." With all the gravity and menace of a Prussian staff officer surveying a battlefield, Madame Sebastian carefully lights and inhales on a cigarette. Fearful of this information reaching their Nazi house guests, who would kill them, the pair decide to poison Alicia slowly.

When Alicia's health begins to wane, Devlin's overt regard for her grows and in a rash, uncharacteristic act he barges into the Sebastian town house to free her from her poisoners. Not only is Devlin acting out of character, but he is also violating his orders, since he has been relieved of his duties in the Huberman case. Devlin is able to exploit the tension between Sebastian and the Nazi Erich, since Sebastian is afraid to expose Devlin's or Alicia's real role and has to walk them to the car for her trip to the hospital. Sebastian is left literally on the doorstep, while Erich watches and waits from the interior of the house.

Notorious may have been a welcome change from the woman as mere passive object in the espionage game, but Alicia was not only motivated to become a spy because of her love for Devlin, it was her danger that prompted his real display of love and concern. Her efficiency as a spy, her ability to appear Sebastian's lover, almost ended their romance, while her peril insured its happy conclusion.

ander has invited Alicia, she notices that one of the guests, a German chemist, is nervous about one of the bottles on the sideboard. Erich (Ivan Triesault), the ostensible leader of the refugee Nazis and scientists has noticed as well, and the chemist dies in an off-screen auto accident. Whatever the exact nature of their conspiracy, they are playing for keeps.

For his part, Sebastian is taken with Alicia, who has made a poor impression on his suspicious mother; she criticizes his lovestruck credulity and fears that Alicia is a simple gold-digger. Sebastian's only fear is the occasional but annoying presence of a young airline executive whom Alicia had met on the flight from Miami, a Mr. Devlin. The major crisis in the frustrated romance between Devlin and Alicia revolves around Sebastian's offer of marriage to the volunteer agent. Upset over the impending mariage, Devlin openly expresses his anger when one of his superiors

The attentive husband, Sebastian (left, Claude Rains), inquires after the health of the wife, Alicia (Ingrid Bergman), whom he has been slowly poisoning, while a Nazi refugee, Dr. Anderson (Reinhold Schunzel), looks on. *(Notorious)*

The espionage involved was deliberately vague: a bottle full of uranium ore and several refugee German scientists flitting about in dinner jackets could have added up to an atomic bomb project somewhere in the Brazilian mountains, but Hecht's screenplay kept the intrigue at the level of a simple plot device, a "MacGuffin," in Hitchcock's word. If romance could eclipse spycraft, even the last world war was not totally immune, and in one 1947 film the demands of British Military Intelligence could take second place to the love affair between Ray Milland and Marlene Dietrich in *Golden Earrings*.

Directed by Mitchell Leisen, this Paramount film was framed by an external narration on screen supplied by war correspondent Quentin Reynolds, who wonders why an ostensibly upper-class British officer, Colonel Ralph Denistoun (Ray Milland), wears a golden earring in one ear. The explanation lay in a flashback of a wartime mission in Germany. Escaping from the Germans, Denistoun

An escaped Colonel Denistoun (Ray Milland) makes sure that Lydia (Marlene Dietrich) will not betray him to the Germans. *(Golden Earrings)*

fell in with a troupe of gypsies, one of whom, Lydia (Marlene Dietrich), literally took him under her wing. She not only dressed him in gypsy clothing, she also tinted his skin and taught him how to tell fortunes, so he could pass himself off as a gypsy in Germany. As a despised minority in Europe and particularly hated by the Nazis, the gypsies were depicted as insulted and harrassed by police and army patrols, but this aspect of the film was consciously eviscerated, according to Abraham Polonsky, one of the three writers who worked on the screenplay.

As a gypsy, Denistoun not only lived with Lydia in her horse-drawn wagon, he also had to fight with Zoltan (Murvyn Vye) to stay with the troupe and began actually to see the future in his friend's palm. As gypsies, Lydia, he and the rest were asked to amuse a gathering of German officers and scientists, and in that way, Denistoun was able to discover the poison gas formula that had been his assignment. At the conclusion of the flashback, he takes his leave of Lydia on a hilltop in France, the same spot that appears at the film's close when a reunited Lydia and Denistoun set off toward the sunset in her little wagon. Romance had finally conquered reality in this vision of wartime espionage.

The romantic espionage tale was one of the cinematic victims of the Cold War; only in comedies was one spy allowed to fall in love with another. In the more serious spy films the romance was either an extra incitement to the protagonist, as in *North-by-Northwest,* or a complex twist in the spy masters' plot, as in *The Spy Who Came in from the Cold.* In the poorly crafted films, sexuality replaced romance; bare female torsos became as standard a visual component as silencer-equipped automatics, and many advertisements shamelessly exploited the Freudian possibilities, particularly the Matt Helm–Dean Martin films. This apparent pornography raised the question of sexual double-standards. Both Mata Hari and X-27 had to bear the burden of seductresses even more than the taint of espionage, while James Bond could jump in and out of bed with any number of beautiful enemy spies without the threat of moral censure or official suspicion. The woman agent could flirt with the enemy only if she had fallen in love with her male ally and was helping him, e.g. Elsa in *Secret Agent.* Emotions, of course, could have little place in the wars waged by spies and their organizations; it was all a matter of national security and Machiavellian complexity. Increasingly, however, the espionage war seemed more a problem of official insanity and psychotic intensity.

"Yes, there will be a war," a disguised Denistoun (Ray Milland) tells the corporal who has asked to have his palm read. (*Golden Earrings*)

170

7

The Edge of Paranoia

Ministry of Fear
The Manchurian Candidate
The Quiller Memorandum
The Parallax View
Escape to Nowhere
The Killer Elite

Each spy worked in a realm pervaded by doubt and mystery; even James Bond had to discover the archfiend's secret laboratory, and sometimes accompanied by unreasonable fears and insurmountable panic both Alec Leamas and Richard Hannay learned the price of misplaced trust, but at the film's end both protagonist and audience realized the underlying logic. Despite apparent contradictions, fiendish doublecrosses and sheer implausibilities, there appeared at the end of ninety minutes a clear rationale. There was, however, another tradition in the spy film, the sordid and lethal conspiracy without logic or motive. Fritz Lang's *Spies,* in a studied disregard of politics or motives, depicted a maddening series of plots and thefts engineered seemingly at the whim of the spy master, Haghi. That particular vision of espionage soon disappeared from the popular screen, although there were occasional traces of neuroses in the villainous spies who filled the screen, notably Peter Lorre's highly strung agents and Sydney Greenstreet's fatalistic conspirators. Madness, sheer psychopathology,

did emerge as a plot device in one of Fritz Lang's wartime films, *Ministry of Fear,* adapted from the Grahame Green novel by the producer, Seton Miller.

Shadowy uncertainty was the hallmark of this 1944 film produced for Paramount. From its very opening scenes of a gloomy bedroom with a barred window, the film had the visual overtones of the German silent film era, while the sound track carried the amplified ticking of a clock and Stephen Neale (Ray Milland) muttering about his freedom. As Neale passes the building's entrance, the audience learns that he has just been released from the Lembridge Asylum. Eager to immerse himself in the crowded life of London, Neale immediately goes to the train station to purchase a third-class, one-way ticket. Warned by the clerk of both a delay in the schedule and a possible air raid, Neale sees a small local carnival being sponsored by a group called the Mothers of the Free Nations and eagerly walks down its midway. He is soon talked into visiting the fortune teller's tent where an English dowager, Mrs. Bellaire (Aminta Dyne), whose

During a costume party, Shaw's mother (Angela Lansbury) waits for her son to reach the exact playing card that will open him to any suggestion. *(The Manchurian Candidate)*

The blind man (Eustace Wyatt) takes aim at a pursuing Neale, in *Ministry of Fear*.

palm he literally crosses with silver, asks him a nondescript question about his life. Responding with a cryptic comment on his recent release, Neale has accidentally given the woman the coded response for which she had been waiting. In turn, she tells him the exact weight of the cake being given away by the carnival hostesses. Neale easily wins the prize, a cake he is reminded that has been made with real eggs, but not before he is challenged by a late-comer who has rushed into the fortune-teller's tent before making an abortive bid for the cake.

Finally on his train to London, Neale is joined by a blind man with whom he shares the cake. Neale notices, however, that the man merely crumbles his portion of the cake and while Neale is distracted by the beginning of an air raid, the blind man clubs him and makes off with the rest of the cake. Pursued by Neale, the man even takes a few potshots at him before being blown up by a stray German bomb. Dazed and fretful as to why he should be the target of an apparent killer, Neale returns to the train and once in London not only contacts a private detective named Rennit, but also visits the headquarters of the Mothers of the Free Nations. There he meets Carla and Willi Hilfe (Marjorie Reynolds and Carl Es-

mond), sister and brother refugees from Vienna, who listen sympathetically to his story and seem eager to solve his mystery. They decide to visit the fortune-telling Mrs. Bellaire to discover the secret behind the mysteriously coveted cake. The Mrs. Bellaire to whom Neale is introduced, however, bears no resemblance to the dowdy woman who had given him the carnival prize but is an elegantly dressed beauty (Hillary Brooke) preparing to host a seance in her London town house. Invited to take part, Neale and the Hilfes are introduced to their colleagues in a sequence of shots that hints at intrigue, hostility, superficial amiability, as well as official interest, since one of the participants, Dr. Forrester (Alan Napier), is a psychologist connected to a secret government ministry which gave the film its title. A late arrival at the seance, a Mr. Cost (Dan Duryea), is also the man who has tried to win the cake from Neale at the carnival, but his attempt at explanation to the Hilfes is silenced—the seance is about to start.

With suitable lighting and eerie music, the spiritualist speaks of murders and madness, while a simulated voice, that of a murdered woman, seeks out one of the participants, and Neale, unnerved by the voice, begins to shout of his innocence and actually breaks the circle of participants. About the same time a shot is heard, and when the lights come on Cost is lying on the floor while Neale stands over him with a gun in his hand. While Forrester and the others go to call the police, the Hilfes, sympathetic to Neale, let him escape. Rushing to Rennit's office, he finds it ransacked and is forced to rely for help on the only other person in London whom he trusts, Carla Hilfe (a rather obvious pun on the German meaning of her name). In an attempt to escape being followed by a man in a black suit and bowler hat, Neale and Carla hide with hundreds of others in an underground station during an air raid, during which Lang's camera details the people preparing to spend the night there in their pajamas, while others bring their bedding down into the shelter with them. The raid also provides the setting and excuse for Neale to disclose why he had been so upset by the seance; he had been sentenced to an asylum following the death of his fatally ill wife; she had died from an overdose of pills, and he was suspected of mercy killing. After the raid Carla takes him to one of her friends, a bookseller, for safety, but Neale is

growing suspicious since there have been no news reports of Cost's death and he begins to suspect some wider conspiracy.

As a favor to the bookseller, Neale and Carla take a briefcase of books to Dr. Forrester's apartment. Forrester, however, is not there, nor is his name on the door. Neale senses a potential trap, but it is too late—the briefcase explodes as he flings himself over Carla to protect her from the blast. When Neale regains consciousness, he is lying in a hospital bed while in a nearby chair sits the man in the black suit and bowler brandishing a penknife. The man turns out to be not a German spy, as Neale had feared, but a Scotland Yard detective who wants to question him about a murder, the murder not of Cost, but of Rennit. Neale's explanation takes him and a squad of police to the place where the blind man had died. Although dubious, the police begin the tedious search for clues, going so far as to sift the dirt for traces of the cake and what it may have contained. Several minutes of screen time are expended on this sequence, since Lang wanted to demonstrate the routine of police work and as the sequence develops the

Soviet troops carry the drugged U.S. Army platoon to the waiting helicopters. *(The Manchurian Candidate)*

Bennett Marco (left, Frank Sinatra) and Raymond Shaw (Laurence Harvey) endure their display as the brainwashed laboratory specimens of the Communists. *(The Manchurian Candidate)*

police strip their jackets and vests and roll up their sleeves, but find nothing. About to be taken back to "the Yard" for questioning, Neale himself starts scrambling around and finds a vial of microfilm in a pigeon's nest near the bomb crater. With this piece of evidence the police realize that Neale has stumbled upon an important spy network whose agents sit on the Ministry of Fear.

Neale's history had, of course, been known to the spies who had tried to frighten him away with the simulated death of Cost at the seance. Even the helpful, friendly Willy was part of the conspiracy, and is finally revealed at the film's end as the ring leader of the spy network.

Although the protagonist's paranoia was used as a dramatic device in *Ministry of Fear,* the situation was relatively clear to its audience. By the sixties, however, solutions did not come as easily to the harried victim–heroes. Even when the opponents seemed distinct, methods and conspiracies were concocted in a deliberate haze. The Korean War provided the background to the 1962 film, *The Manchurian Candidate,* in which the prime character was both victim and antagonist, a specially trained assassin who really *was* his cover until literally activated by his control. The Korean

War was barely a decade old and there was enough popular fascination with the process of brainwashing that the film scripted by George Axelrod from Richard Condon's novel achieved a great deal of notoriety. It also raised the psychological dilemma of the enemy agent who didn't know he was one.

In keeping with this awesome premise the film actually opens with a nightmare, the same dream as experienced by a number of GI's who had escaped capture by North Korean troops during the war. The fact was, of course, that they had not really escaped, but only their unconscious memories remember the special psychological programming to which they had been subjected at an institute somewhere on the Sino-Soviet border. The dream consisted of being on some sort of stage watched by an assembly of Korean, Chinese and Russian officers while they are interviewed and introduced by a tall, bald official named Yen Lo (Khigh Dhiegh), who calmly suggests that Raymond Shaw (Laurence Harvey), one of the captured soldiers, shoot the platoon's favorite, youngest member. Without a quiver, Shaw blows his brains out, there is a splattering of blood on the huge portrait of Stalin adorning the stage, and the nightmare is ended. When questioned about their reaction to Shaw, all the men respond with the same formula, that Shaw is one of the greatest human beings they'd ever met. Besides being the psychologically prepared assassin, Shaw had also been groomed as the platoon's hero, the man who had liberated the platoon from its Korean captors, and a Congressional Medal of Honor winner. The triggering device for Shaw was the suggestion that he play solitaire, since the appearance of the queen of diamonds opened him to any suggestion.

A journalist based in Washington, D.C., Shaw had been assigned two agents to watch over him, his valet, a Korean, Chunjim (Henry Silva), and by far the more important one, his own mother (Angela Lansbury). A domineering, ambitious woman, she was also a dedicated Communist agent who could discuss with obvious pride the skillful conspiracy by which her husband, a right-wing politician would become president. However, her ambition exceeded the demands of the Communists, since she harbored a bitter resentment over their use of her son as a tool in the conspiracy; indeed, she expressed threats to take revenge on the Soviets for their turning him into a killing machine. The film's action was based on a truly maddening set of circumstances: that a man could be programmed into an assassin by the sight of a playing card, that a right-wing political crusade could mask a Communist bid for power and that the personal dynamics between the programmed killer and his family could prove part of the conspiracy's potential drawbacks.

Curiously enough, Shaw is normally repelled by his parents' virulent anti-communism and is reluctant to let them use him as a be-medalled example of their views. He has even become romantically involved with the daughter of one of their political foes, Senator Thomas Jordan (John McGiver). Unable to allow this danger to her plans (and perhaps a thinly veiled attack by a dominant maternal figure), Shaw's mother triggers him to kill both his future wife and father-in-law. This murder not only forces Shaw to rely more upon his mother, but it also focusses growing attention on his step-father's political cam-

Shaw's girlfriend, Jocie Jordan (Leslie Parrish), has accidentally chosen the costume most likely to make a hit with the brainwashed reporter (Laurence Harvey). *(The Manchurian Candidate)*

paign. The mysterious, motive-less killings also prompt Shaw's wartime officer, Major Marco (Frank Sinatra), to investigate the background to his and the other GIs' nightmare. When he visits Shaw, the major meets the Korean valet, whom he remembers as the man who had led the platoon into the ambush. This encounter and the strange similarity surrounding each man's memory of the incident in Korea force Marco to try to piece together the various parts of the puzzle.

If Marco is beginning to understand the basis for his and the other men's recurring nightmares, the Communists are preparing the final mechanism in their plot—Shaw. At a private clinic in upstate New York, he is being re-programmed by Yen Lo and his Soviet technicians. Lo is depicted as a totally cynical manipulator; he laughingly tells the clinic's

177

Shortly before they are both to be shot, Mrs. Shaw (Angela Lansbury) confers with Senator John Iselin (James Gregory), during the political convention at the film's climax. *(The Manchurian Candidate)*

Russian director that he should worry that as head of one of the few profitable Soviet front operations in North America, he could be considered a capitalist. A humorous version of Dr. Fu Manchu, complete to a long Mongolian-style moustache, Lo even mentions the shopping list his wife had given him as prelude to his visit to America. Shaw's task is to assassinate the Presidential nominee during the political convention at Madison Square Garden, thus paving the way for his parents' legal bid for power. During the film's final sequence, as Marco begins the long ascent to the ceiling-high booth where Shaw is stationed, the unwilling assassin prepares to fire, but whether because of Marco's coded phrase or his own realization, he shoots his parents, then puts on his Congressional Medal of Honor and in front of a terrified Marco blows his own brains out.

The Manchurian Candidate's conspiratorial view of foreign intrigue was unabashedly psychopathic. Besides the use of a robot-like, unconscious agent, the film posited a political gimmick that was designed to appeal to both liberals and right-wingers, with a hero everyone could like. The virulent right-wing anticommunists were shown to be actual agents and spies, so that one portion of the audience could rest assured that patriotism was indeed a screen for its opposite, and the other portion could remain justified in their claims for the Communists' duplicity. Yen Lo added the necessary dash of inscrutable Manchurian cynicism, while Shaw's mother prompted whole discussions of the changing characterization of the American maternal image. There were even hints of Sino-Soviet rivalry in the opening scenes of the captured platoon on display before its psychological trainers.

What was exceptional, of course, was the idea of spy as robot, as a real victim forced without his knowledge or will to carry out orders of which he has no conscious idea. Although a foolproof spy without nerves, fears or regrets, Shaw was also more of a machine than a human being; it was only at the film's climax that his dilemma became interesting. The literal dehumanization of the agent or spy was not only the logical extension of paranoia; since nobody could know whether he had been programmed or not, everyone was a potential spy or assassin. It also could mean the end of the spy film. After all, human weaknesses and delusions were as much a part of the spy's trade as secret cameras and automatic pistols. It was the mixture of human and ahuman in the spy's normal character that made him interesting, a source for modern novelists and filmmakers; "the soul of the spy," the critic and scholar Jacques Barzun had written more than a decade ago, "is somehow the model of our own." The fully human spy who had knowingly accepted his mission and its dangers only to realize at its end the ultimate futility and aimlessness of his work

Quiller (George Segal) has been secretly drugged; he will soon be taken to the neo-Nazi headquarters he has sought. *(The Quiller Memorandum)*

Max Von Sydow as Oktober, the Reichs-führer of the neo-Nazis. *(The Quiller Memorandum)*

was the ideal symptom of societal insanity.

The search for neo-Nazis in postwar Berlin would seem the last topic for futility or cycnicism, yet as scripted by Harold Pinter from the novel by Adam Hall, *The Quiller Memorandum* depicted an espionage assignment that not only seemed to end as a failure, but a task that was designed without the prospect of success. Adding to this tone of despair was the casting of George Segal in the role of Quiller, an American-educated British spy whose relationship to his control, the stodgy Englishman, Pol (Alec Guinness), was a shade below outright hostility. Quiller had accepted the mission of locating the neo-Nazis since another spy, his friend, had been murdered by them at the film's opening. In his search for clues, Quiller contacts the dead agent's girl friend, a German schoolteacher, Inge (Senta Berger), whose friends included a former member of the neo-Nazi circle. Quiller's relationship to Inge was a critical element in the film, since it not only served as a pivot for the action, but also reversed the traditional pattern of romance in the spy film.

Quiller eventually meets the neo-Nazis and their leader, Oktober (Max Von Sydow), who is respectfully addressed by his subordinates as "Reichsführer," a reference to Oktober's rank in the past/present hierarchy.

Drugged with different substances to gain information about his control's name and location, Quiller manages to confuse his answers with references to Inge, so that Oktober learns nothing. Whether a ruse or an honest mistake, Quiller is left abandoned near one of the rivers that divide Berlin and reports his contact with the enemy to Pol. Like the "Reichsfuhrer" Pol was mainly interested in finding the exact location of his enemy's headquarters, since that was a clue to the identity of all their agents in Berlin. Using a luncheon bun as illustration, Pol coolly tells Quiller that he is in the middle of the fog that separated the two opponents while in contact with both. Using Inge's friend as a guide, Quiller locates the near-derelict mansion that serves as Oktober's base. Captured a second time by Oktober's lieutenants, Quiller is calmly released; Inge is being held as a hostage and Oktober's men are openly following Quiller to discover Pol's headquarters. Through car chases, taxi switches and an abortive time bomb explosion, Quiller manages to reach Pol in his office overlooking West Berlin's Kufürstendamm. The neo-Nazi headquarters have been raided and Pol is pleased enough to offer nonchalantly that Quiller accompany him for breakfast. Quiller, tired from his dawn race with Oktober's thugs and worried about Inge, bluntly refuses. The po-

"You are the man in the middle," Pol (right, Alec Guinness) tells his agent, Quiller (George Segal). *(The Quiller Memorandum)*

lice report on the raid mentions nothing about a female prisoner among their catch, and the next morning Quiller goes to the school where he had first met her. She is there, alive and unharmed, leading her charges back to the classroom, as they sing a children's song. As Quiller stares at her, the only noise on the sound track is the song, a cheerful yet ominous hint of the future.

The Quiller Memorandum had many of the merits of the traditional spy film: the suspense and adventure of hunting down Nazis twenty years after the war in the seat of their former glory, the confrontation of rivals who seemed equally well-organized and ruthless, the tensions between the Anglo-American Quiller and his haughty superior, the machinations in London of politicians like Gibbs (George Sanders), who engineer the spy war and the ambiguous romance between Quiller and Inge. The uncertainty of that affair was key to the sense of futility surrounding Quiller's assignment. Was Inge a born survivor, a neo-Nazi used to romance the opposition or a double-agent working for yet another side? Despite his apparent success, his skill in evading Okto-

Whether left for dead or left with a warning, Quiller (George Segal) has clambered out of a Berlin river, only to have to face an unfriendly barkeeper. *(The Quiller Memorandum)*

Oktober (Max Von Sydow) is relying upon Inge (Senta Berger), as the guarantee of Quiller's harmlessness. *(The Quiller Memorandum)*

ber's trap, Quiller was left, as was the audience, with the feeling that the entire mission had been futile and meaningless. Underlying the film and particularly because of the casting of Segal in the title role, was a feeling that espionage was a horrid exercise, performed merely for the sake of form and the employment of highly placed officials and alienated adventurers. This desperation or failure of nerve on the part of the spy had been an important, though fleeting, ingredient of Hitchcock's *Secret Agent,* but was becoming the major theme of more modern spy films. Leamas at the conclusion of *The Spy Who Came in from the Cold* knew, at least, the background reasons for the intrigue that cost Nan's life and for which he sacrificed his own; Quiller and the audience were left ignorant of the real logic, if any, for his mission and of the feelings remaining between him and Inge. Isolation, despair and futility seemed to have replaced the adventure, drama and patriotism of espionage.

In 1974 an American filmmaker, Alan

Quiller (George Segal) discovers the time bomb Oktober's men have planted on his car. *(The Quiller Memorandum)*

182

Warren Beatty and Paula Prentiss.
(The Parallax View)

Pakula, reproduced this feeling of victimization in a story that was built around a series of political assassinations. *The Parallax View* began with the mysterious assassination of a popular senator at a July 4th political rally. One of the witnesses to the murder is a cynical reporter, Joe Frady (Warren Beatty), who is soon pressured into discovering and interviewing the steadily dwindling number of other witnesses. Not merely an abstract interest, his quest has been prompted by the death, under accidental circumstances, of course, of another witness, his ex-lover Lee Carter (Paula Prentiss). Herself a TV reporter, she had spoken to him about a conspiracy shortly before her auto accident and showed him a blown-up photograph taken before the assassin's shot of two waiters, only one of whom had been indentified.

Following up a lead Lee has given him, Frady begins questioning a local sheriff about the drowning death of one of the more important witnesses. Investigating the site of the man's death, Frady is himself almost murdered by the sheriff, who has lured him into the path of a dam's sluice. This attempted murder not only alerts Frady to a real connection between the deaths of the various wit-

Face-off between suspected assassin and detectives atop Seattle's Space Needle in the initial sequences of *The Parallax View*.

A visit from Lee (center, Paula Prentiss) interrupts Frady's (Warren Beatty) morning with Chrissy (left, Joanne Harris). (*The Parallax View*)

nesses, but also supplies the reporter with a new clue. Amid the sheriff's papers, he finds an employment application from the Parallax Corporation. Taking advantage of his friends at a psychological clinic, Frady learns that the application has been designed to select psychotic individuals with violent histories. Having had the form filled out by one of the clinic's patients, Frady obtains false identification from an ex-FBI pal and waits for the Parallax Corporation to contact him in a shabby boarding house. They soon do.

Acting sullen and suspicious, Frady is told that his talents are needed by the corporation, and a sleek, calm emissary not only gives him some money but also tells him of his next interview at the corporation's offices. Before he goes, however, Frady gives his paper's editor, Bill Rintels (Hume Cronyn), a tape of the recording he has made of his initial interview.

Television news commentator Lee Carter (left, Paula Prentiss) interviews senatorial aide Austin (right, William Daniels), while newspaper reporter Joe Frady (far right, Warren Beatty) prepares to crash the reception. (*The Parallax View*)

Cocktail waitress Gale (Doria Cook) introduces herself to Frady (Warren Beatty). *(The Parallax View)*

Lee Carter (right, Paula Prentiss) brings Frady (Warren Beatty) evidence of a conspiracy to eliminate witnesses to the assassination. *(The Parallax View)*

Disregarding Rintels' warnings, Frady continues his search for the real murderers and a potential Pulitzer Prize. Before that reward, however, he has to take the psychological test designed by the Parallax Corporation.

Summoned to a cavernous auditorium in a super-futuristic office building, Frady sees neither executives nor secretaries, let alone other applicants; he only hears a recorded feminine voice inviting him to take the solitary seat in the darkened room. The test consists of a slide show on a huge screen with super-stereophonic sound geared to the theme and pacing of the changing slides. Typical symbols of love, nature and maternity are contrasted with equally traditional scenes of loneliness, sex and violence, but the mix of symbols and the pacing changes abruptly, until love is soon equated with violence. The entire screen is taken up by the slides, so that it is not only Frady who is undergoing this test, but the audience as well. An altogether untraditional sequence, neither Frady nor the audience knows whether he has passed this survey, and neither knows what success means in terms of the Parallax Corporation. Leaving the building, he soon sees a familiar face, the mysterious waiter, the potential assassin (Chuck Waters).

Following the man to a nearby airport, Frady sees him check a suitcase aboard a flight

Barroom brawl between Frady (left, Warren Beatty) and Red (Earl Hindman). *(The Parallax View)*

185

Joe Frady (left, Warren Beatty), about to be baited by the local deputy sheriff and bully, Red (Earl Hindman). *(The Parallax View)*

Warren Beatty as Joe Frady, reporter turned investigator in *The Parallax View.*

that he doesn't board, but Frady does. Learning that a senator is on board, Frady must warn the pilot without exposing himself as the informer. Rather than leave a message written on the bathroom mirror, Frady hits upon the clever trick of slipping a message into the pile of napkins on the stewardess' cocktail wagon. The bomb which he has feverishly anticipated does indeed explode, as he and his fellow pas-

Frady (right, Warren Beatty) snares not only his would-be murderer, the sheriff (Kelly Thordsen), but also his first real clue. *(The Parallax View)*

Reporter Joe Frady (right, Warren Beatty) is contacted by Austin's bodyguard (Bill Jordan). *(The Parallax View)*

At a meet in a children's playground, Frady (Warren Beatty) asks former FBI man Turner (left, Kenneth Mars) for phony identification papers. *(The Parallax View)*

sengers are leaving the airstrip to which the plane has returned. Frady now knows for sure that the Parallax Corporation rents out assassins, but the ground on which he is standing, his room for maneuver, is narrowing. The man who had left the timebomb, the assassin from the first murder, appears one night as the delivery man with Rintels' midnight snack. Having poisoned the editor, the assassin also erases Frady's taped interview with the Parallax Corporation representative. When Frady goes to learn his assignment from them, the professional assassins have already destroyed his link to the outside world.

A reclusive Austin (left, William Daniels) grants an interview to Frady (right, Warren Beatty), while a guard (Bill Jordan) looks on. *(The Parallax View)*

Warren Beatty as Joe Frady, reporter. *(The Parallax View)*

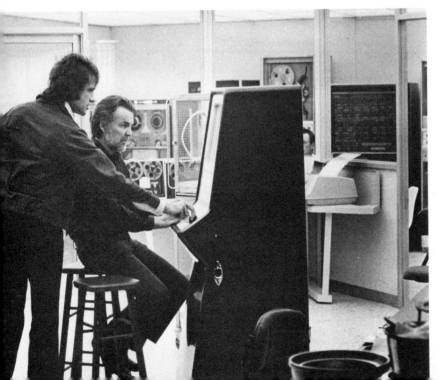

Filling out the Parallax Corporation questionnaire, Frady (Warren Beatty) gets help from psychological researcher Schwartzkopf (right, Anthony Zerbe). *(The Parallax View)*

189

In a shabby boarding house, Parallax Corporation recruiter Jack (right, Walter McGinn) meets applicant Frady (Warren Beatty). *(The Parallax View)*

Arriving early at the hotel where he is scheduled to meet his partner, Frady catches a glimpse of the sheriff's deputy from his earlier misadventure near the dam. In a good attempt at foiling the trap he senses, Frady sends the deputy out of the city with a supposed change of orders from the corporation. It seems that Frady was about to discover the exact nature of his assignment without risk, until the camera glimpses anonymous men in business suits carrying walkie-talkies and wearing lapel tags that read "Security." These rapid close-ups turn into the rehearsal preparations for yet another senatorial candidate, another victim for an unseen assassin's bullet. On the catwalks overlooking the convention

Frady (Warren Beatty) searches for the likely victim on the shuttle flight; he finds him in the first-class section. *(The Parallax View)*

Newspaper editor Ben Rintels (center, Hume Cronyn) and police detective (right, Robert Lieb) hear Frady (Warren Beatty) explain his tactics for solving the mysterious assassinations. *(The Parallax View)*

center, Frady tries to pursue the assassin, only dimly aware that he is more the quarry than the hunter. Frady is shot and his body delivered up to the authorities as the suspected assassin.

Scripted by David Giler and Lorenzo Semple, Jr., the film closed as it had opened, with an official-looking panel of jurists who have declared any charges of conspiracy arising from the events just shown to be unwarranted. Coming within a decade marked by political assassinations, *The Parallax View* gave audiences a subjective view of the myths, reports and rumors surrounding the deaths of the Kennedys, Martin Luther King and Malcolm X. Although there were no reasons or motives given for the murders in the film, the theme was obvious, that the supposed assas-

Parallax Corporation representative Jack (Walter McGinn) explains instructions to Frady (right, Warren Beatty). *(The Parallax View)*

Bill Rintels (Hume Cronyn), Frady's editor, warns him of danger ahead. (The Parallax View)

Joe Frady (Warren Beatty) phones ahead to avoid any trap planned by the Parallax Corporation. *(The Parallax View)*

sins were only decoys, fall-guys, especially selected and trapped by an efficiently organized group. Except for the waiter and the initial contact man from Parallax, neither viewers nor Frady learned who the exact antagonists were; they were either unseen or glimpsed only in nondescript action sequences. Frady didn't even get a good look at his final assailant. This emphasis on the psychological and personal, the antithesis of the other film that dealt with the Kennedy assassination directly, *Executive Action,* pointed to an aura of organized insanity in which the brave, sane individual was not only helpless, but used to further political murder.

The hunter-hunted, Frady (Warren Beatty), hides from Parallax security man (Glenn Wilder) in catwalk above Convention Center. *(The Parallax View)*

Politically motivated murder was nothing new to Europe, where people had experienced the activities of at least four of the modern world's most well-known espionage networks: the British, German, American and Russian. Faced by a state apparatus that was both remorseless and inexorable, the lone individual became a simple victim, no matter how long the inevitable fate was delayed. Lies, deceptions, kidnappings and murders became not only methods used by governments, but were honed to a point of perfection. A kidnapping opened the 1974 French film, *Escape to Nowhere (Le Silencieux),* moreover, a kidnapping in what has been accepted as the least exciting European capital, London.

On his way home from the theater, a Soviet scientist, Haliakov (Lino Ventura), escorted by his KGB guards, is deftly snatched by agents of the British Secret Service. Brought before a group of British operatives, he is questioned by their chief (Leo Genn), so that Haliakov's full story is revealed. A physicist who had originally been born Clement Tibere, Haliakov has not only worked for the British during the war, but had been initially abducted by the Russians more than 15 years ago! Now, back in London, the British are sure that Haliakov/Tibere would not only be pleased to be back in the Free World, but to repay the British with information about two Soviet agents. The physicist refuses; he tells them that he is not willing to be gunned down

The man called Haliakov (center, Lino Ventura) knows that the London ambulance men do mean him harm. *(Escape to Nowhere)*

in revenge by the KGB. The stolid English faces, however, reveal the alternative: if he *doesn't* tell them the names, he will be shot by British Intelligence. Staring at his saviors, Haliakov/Tibere can honestly tell them, "You are the other side."

In return for his information, the British give him a set of phony identification, some money, a gun, and what is perhaps the most important, a counter with which to bargain with the KGB—the name of a Soviet agent, a classical musician, sought by the French security services. From this point on, the film, directed by Claude Pinotheau, was almost two spy stories revolving around its main protagonist, since he must not only avoid the KGB killers on his trail, but must also threaten the security of the Soviet agent. The scientist may have had the experience of a wartime Resistance fighter, but he is now twenty years older and unused to the strain of the spy's field work. Still, he has not forgotten the necessary procedures. Hiding out in a small hotel room from which he can view the street, he not only providentially remembers to pull the shades down before going to bed, but more importantly remembers *not* to raise them in the morning. Leaving the hotel neither by the front door nor a side entrance but through the attic, he hears the telltale shot when the clerk mechanically opens the window for the morning air and becomes a waiting marksman's target.

Haliakov/Tibere is not only a hunted man; he is also displaced in time and space. All

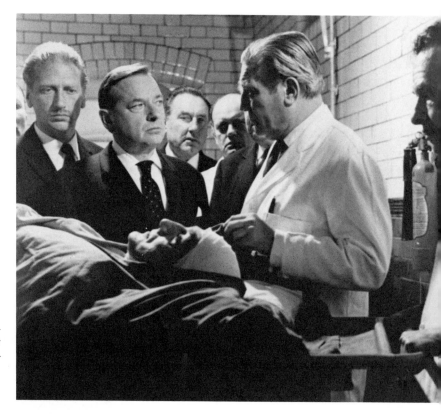

The British secret-service men examine their latest catch, Haliakov (on stretcher, Lino Ventura). *(Escape to Nowhere)*

of his acquaintances in Western Europe were fifteen years out of date, and had he sought them out, he knew he might endanger them as well. Still, he manages to incriminate the Soviet musician, whose scores are peppered with microdots, but he is unable to evade the KGB's revenge. From London through France to an isolated spot in the foothills of the Swiss Alps, the team of KGB gunmen have followed their quarry, and the airborne camera shows an exhausted man being coverged on by several armed assailants while a voice-over tells the audience that the man named Haliakov was not killed, but merely crippled with gunshots for having breached Soviet security.

What made *Escape to Nowhere* different was that the protagonist was depicted as a totally normal human being. He had grown used to a scientist's life in Russia and was not used to being a spy. His labored breathing on the sound track, the look of weary exhaustion and fear on his face and his remorse about not being able to say hello to his grown-up daughter were marks of individuality that contrasted nicely with the anonymous men after him.

This view of humanity as hapless, hamstrung victims was not new to literature, of course, but few spy films had dared to picture the total ruthlessness of espionage so personally. Haliakov/Tibere was not one of Hitchcock's cheerful heroes forced by circumstances and a beautiful girl into playing at being a spy, but an unwilling, though not unwitting, tool in the hands of the spy masters. That actual foreign interests were involved, the KGB, MI-5 and the Sureté, only gave the film's plot some plausibility. A later French production did not bother with supposed foreign agents, but had its protagonist hunted down by his own countrymen.

The Secret (Le Secret), released in 1975, opened with a scene of methodical torture. Strapped to a bed in either a hospital or secret police prison (there is little distinction between

One dead agent and one survivor, Haliakov (right, Lino Ventura). *(Escape to Nowhere)*

the two in the paranoiac view of life), a man, David (Jean-Louis Trintignant), has his forehead exposed to a controlled water torture, a steady drip on the head which is amplified and magnified by the camera and sound track. Somehow, David manages to slug his guard/orderly and escape with the man's identity papers and make his way to an isolated part of France. In the apparently abandoned relic of a farmhouse, he comes across a couple, Julia and Thomas (Marlene Jobert and Phillipe Noiret), to whom he tells his story. David, a journalist, has discovered "the secret" which

David (right, Jean-Louis Trintignant) grapples with Thomas (Philippe Noiret). *(The Secret)*

One small street battle, in which Jerome Miller (Bo Hopkins) demonstrates his skill with an Uzi submachine gun. *(The Killer Elite)*

the government was protecting at all costs, even the cost of his life and sanity. Alternately interested and terrified by David, the couple decide to help him. In one of the few amusing sequences in this grim film by Robert Enrico and Pascal Jardin, David's warning of official threat is followed by the sudden appearance of military helicopters and a company of troops with armored equipment. The troops and their commander, however, are just as surprised as Julia and Thomas, since they had thought the terrain for maneuvers was unoccupied.

Although Thomas agrees to help David get to Spain, Julia is growing suspicious; she has seen his phony identity papers and is told by the police that a dangerous madman has recently escaped from a military hospital. She also telephones a reporter friend in Paris to check David's story, and the reporter innocently goes to another friend, a government official. Soon, the audience can see the helicopter hovering over the unwary trio, a symbol of official power and surveillance, a modern angel of doom.

David has not only the government to fear, but Julia as well; she has not only spoken to her Parisian friend but may have also damaged the car taking them to Thomas' boat, the means by which he has promised to take David to Spain. Whether fascinated by David's obsession or in an effort to delay him, Julia even goes so far as to make love with him. This romance, unlike the traditional love element in the spy film, did not signify a happy conclusion but the opposite. Struck by the realization that the plainclothesmen were approaching, David gives Julia his gun as either a symbol of trust or a modern Judas kiss. She shoots him, but her act does not prevent the special police from eliminating her and Thomas. In perhaps the film's only tender scene, Thomas shields his wife's eyes from their approach. And the secret? It lay in the film's final, haunting image —the reporter whom Julia had telephoned was himself a prisoner as David had been in the opening sequence. Whether adversary or unconscious victim, both *Escape to Nowhere* and *The Secret* pointed at the government, any government, as the sanctioned torturer and murderer acting on whim disguised as national security.

Divorced from realistic political needs and motives, espionage became a matter of mere professional expertise and physical endurance: James Bond with the addition of plausible graphic violence. That was the theme in Sam Peckinpah's *The Killer Elite.* From an early scene of call girls hired by a private spy agency to keep its employees happy, through the recuperation from a bullet-shattered arm and knee to a climactic slaughter of the antagonistic henchmen, this 1975 film stressed the theme of amoral, unpolitical expertise. In a curious reversal of values, the sudden revelation of betrayal and the fluctuation of sides—the very basics of espionage—were condemned, while the murderous techniques were applauded. Other filmmakers in an effort to furnish their protagonists or heroic victims with some moralistic footing resuscitated former Nazis and SS men as a plot device (*Marathon Man*), or linked the car chases and shoot-outs to terrorist plots (*Black Sunday*). What had been forgotten was that if spying had nothing at all to do with actual nations and likely situations, the whole of espionage could be reduced to absurdity. Without human motives and fears spycraft was no longer a test of wits and nerve, but an excuse for wisecracks and buffoonery, and that is how many filmmakers have depicted the ancient profession.

The Urge for Humor 8

Pepe (Peter Lorre) and Madame (Judith Anderson) wear their characteristic expressions for their roles in *All Through the Night*.

All Through the Night
My Favorite Blonde
To Be or Not to Be
Our Man in Havana
The Tall Blond Man with One Black Shoe
A Pain in the A**

In any good spy film appearances and reality had to conflict; the obvious enemy agent with thick accent and dressed in a trench coat and slouch hat populated the grade B programmers designed to supply the second half of a double bill at the local theaters. While deception and disguise could lead to intrigue and complexity, it could also lead to outright confusion and slapstick, so that the spy film frequently bordered on tragedy and comedy simultaneously. If no one had been killed in *The 39 Steps* or *The Lady Vanishes*, Hitchcock's two films could be considered witty farces, while the James Bond films might be thought comic in their flagrant disregard of common sense and their caricatured antagonists. Of course, *The Scarlet Pimpernel, The Adventuress, Night Train to Munich* and *Five Graves to Cairo* had their humorous elements, but some directors and writers chose to fashion outright comedies within the demands of the spy film format. King Vidor's *Comrade X,* a 1940 production, featured an American reporter–spy (Clark Gable) whose romance with a stolid Bolshevik streetcar conductor (Hedy Lamarr)

was played against a background of political assassinations and shifts of power in the Kremlin. America's entry into the war spurred the studios to parody the enemy. Some of the wartime films depicted familiar comic groups, Laurel and Hardy or the Bowery Boys, battling it out, not with their traditional adversaries: landlords, wives, bullies and cops, but with Nazi spies and saboteurs. And if the studios could recruit their clowns into the war effort, those other denizens of the screen, the gangsters, could be drafted as well. And what better gangster than Humphrey Bogart as "Gloves" Donahue in *All Through the Night?*

As characterized in the screenplay by Leonard Spigelglass and Edwin Gilbert, "Gloves" was a New York City gambler too hardboiled and cynical to seem much of a hero. However, he has two weaknesses, the desire to please his mother (Jane Darwell), and a fondness for cheese cake as baked by an emigrant German baker. That baker is soon found murdered and Ma Donahue prompts her son and his pal Barney (Frank McHugh) to investigate. The link between the murdered man and his Nazi killers is a woman, nightclub singer Leda Hamilton (Karen Verne), who had been forced to act as a courier to protect her relatives living presumably in Germany as well as in Yorkville. Having met Leda Hamilton, "Gloves" is not only romantically interested, but he also sees the Nazi spy master, Hall Ebbing (Conrad Veidt).

Ebbing is a dignified and elegant antiques dealer who numbers among his assistants the seriously somber Madame (Judith Anderson), who acts as both his secretary and colleague, and the more erratic Pepe (Peter Lorre), as well as the heavily accented platoon of expatriate Germans who played spies and Nazis in hundreds of wartime films: Martin Kosleck, Hans Schumm and Otto Reichow. Besides his suspicions of "Gloves'" real interests, Ebbing is jealous of his interest in Leda and feels he has dismissed the danger when "Gloves" becomes the wanted suspect in the murder of a "business" competitor whom Ebbing has had killed to silence his wavering loyalty.

In his attempt to discover the real killer, "Gloves" discovers the secret room within Eb-

bing's offices, complete to a portrait of Hitler on the wall. Extrapolating from the premise of a secret headquarters, director Vincent Sherman staged a sequence that was the film's comic highlight—a confrontation between American humor and Nazi conspiracy. Having mugged and stolen the identification from two saboteurs, "Gloves" and Barney manage to infiltrate a briefing session by Steindorff (Kosleck) of some three dozen fifth columnists. Called upon to give a report on their work, "Gloves" and Barney improvise, using double-talk, street jargon and shouts of "Heil Hitler," which brings the assembled spies to their feet in salute. At the meeting, the two Americans learn that the Nazis' target was a battleship on its way from the Brooklyn Navy Yard, and to forestall them, "Gloves" and Barney must mobilize their friends into a small army of lovable crooks and silly shysters.

The scene that depicted "Gloves" and his pals discussing the menace posed by Ebbing was a mixture of high school civics and Damon Runyon. When one mobster tells him that there is no difference which government

"Gloves" Donahue (Humphrey Bogart) chats with Leda Hamilton (Karen Verne), while nightclub owner Joe Denning (right, Edward S. Brophy) and Nazi spy Pepe (left, Peter Lorre) prepare to move in. *(All Throught the Night)*

sends its cops to break up their rackets, "Gloves" responds with the notion that there is a world of difference between the occasional legal bust and the form of total rule and control represented by these particular "visitors from across the big pond." By the time he has finished, all his associates and pals, including Starchie, Spats and a favorite waiter (Jackie Gleason, Wallace Ford and Phil Silvers), are ready to lay into the Nazi nest. In the free-for-all fist fight that follows, the would-be saboteurs are soundly beaten, but Ebbing and Pepe manage to escape. In an off-beat, perhaps improvised, scene, Pepe, urged by Ebbing to carry out their assignment to destroy the battleship, refuses and says that it is silly to continue. Ebbing shoots him on the spot, and to show the audience what the New German is capable of, tries to launch his motor boat laden with explosives against the hull of the battleship. "Gloves," having followed Ebbing, prevents this last show of heroic villainy.

Conceived as an outright joke, *All Through the Night* not only served as a model for a far less amusing postwar sequel, *Pick-up on South Street,* but also prompted other studios to parody the enemy within the format of the spy film. One of these films was to become controversial when it was released in 1942 and has since become a favorite among the young and an interesting presage of the "black humor" films that became popular in the 1960's. That film was Ernst Lubitsch's *To Be or Not to Be.* Neatly constructed from a screenplay by Edwin Mayer, this 1942 production from United Artists used the theme of impersonation and the symbiosis between the theatrical and the actual as its motif. The espionage depicted, the retrieval of important documents from an enemy agent, was only the excuse for Lubitsch's exercise in satire.

The film's opening quarter-hour was in itself both a hint of future themes, and a hilarious spoof. While a somber off-screen narrator declares that something has happened to the normal routine of a Warsaw day, the camera reveals a scowling Hitler (Tom Dugan) staring at the window of a local delicatessen. For the

Opening scene: peacetime Warsaw, with the theater featured prominently at rear of set. *(To Be or Not to Be)*

solution to his presence in Poland's capital, the off-screen voice and the visuals take the viewers back to Gestapo headquarters in Berlin, where a Hitler Youth is being plied with war toys by a Gestapo colonel to disclose the little joke his father had made about the Führer. That joke ("they named a champagne after Napoleon, a herring after Bismarck, and Hitler will end up as a piece of cheese") was heard later in the film, but its initial effect was blunted by the sudden appearance at the colonel's office of Hitler himself. To the crisp sound of heel clickings and the hoarse "Heil Hitlers," the German dictator returns the salute and says, "Heil Myself," when stopped by a furious stage director. The entire preceding sequence in the apparent Gestapo office had been a stage play in dress rehearsal. When the director begins to criticize the bit player's makeup as Hitler, the actor, in an effort to prove his resemblance, walks out of the theater into the Warsaw streets. That is how Hitler appeared in Poland in the last summer of peace.

The encounter of Thespian vanity and political reality was the film's central core, although the performers involved were the troupe's stars, Maria and Joseph Tura (Carole Lombard and Jack Benny). The two defended each other from the director's demands for realism: Maria insisted on her right to wear an evening gown in a concentration camp scene, the couple traded quips with each other about their billing on the program and their celebrity status. This debate achieved a high point and soon became a standing joke, as well as the film's title. Fascinated by a young Polish pilot, Sobinski (Robert Stack), who visited her backstage, Maria tells him to visit her when her husband, Joseph, begins his recitation of the famous soliloquy in *Hamlet*. Besides a minor infidelity, her instructions to Sobinski were also a malicious assault on her husband's vanity as an actor. Indeed, he was so outraged by this repeated insult to his performance that Joseph assumes everybody is equally outraged until he is told that they were reacting to the news of the German invasion.

The actors learn that they cannot stage their anti-Nazi play. From left: Bronski (Tom Dugan); Greenberg (Felix Bressart); Kawitch (Lionel Atwill); prompter (Erno Verebes); Joseph Tura (Jack Benny); and Dobosh (Charles Halton). *(To Be or Not to Be)*

Sobinski manages to escape to England to fly with the Polish contingent of the Royal Air Force, and he is seen with his flying companions being visited by a representative of the Polish Government-in-exile, a Professor Siletski (Stanley Ridges). The professor drops a few obvious hints about an impending secret mission to Poland and "reluctantly" collects the names of the pilots' friends and relatives. Eager to contact Maria Tura, Sobinski gives Siletski the phrase "to be or not to be," a code signal about which Siletski was inquisitive. Sobinski proudly mentions Maria Tura's name, but the professor doesn't seem to recognize it. Suspicious, the young pilot goes to MI-5; there the British spy chiefs are concerned. Whether a foolish error on Siletski's part, or proof of his treachery, the British order Sobinski to parachute into occupied Warsaw to prevent the professor from giving the Gestapo the list of the pilots' relatives and friends.

Once back in Warsaw Sobinski stays at the Turas' apartment, a fact Mr. Tura discovers only in the middle of the night. While the pilot-turned-spy and the actor-playing-suspicious-husband try to think of a plan to trap Siletski, the professor has already begun the machinery of the film's comic intrigue; he has sent two German soldiers to bring him Maria

Tura. Siletski's double seduction, political as well as sexual, since he tries to win the actress over to the right side, "the winning side," is curtailed by a midnight call from Gestapo headquarters to see Colonel Erhardt. The headquarters was, of course, the old theater done up in the sets from the play with which the film had opened, and the Nazi colonel was none other than "that great Polish actor, Joseph Tura."

And just as the viewers were drawn into the illusion at the opening, so is Siletski. The ringing telephones, the bustling uniformed officers, the Nazi banners and the city maps fool the enemy agent so completely that Siletski can say that he is pleased to breathe the air of the Gestapo again. The Nazis are all Polish actors, of course, and one of them, Kawitch (Lionel Atwill), cannot pass up the chance to steal a scene; despite the frantic warnings of another actor he proceeds to tell Siletski a short verse about the English lion drinking tea from cups made in Germany. Astounded by such a display in a German officer, Siletski seems mollified when told the man is Göring's brother-in-law.

The film's first real display of mordant humor occurs in the dialogue between Tura, as the Nazi Colonel Erhardt, and Siletski. Told

Maria Tura (Carole Lombard) summoned to German headquarters to see Siletski. *(To Be or Not to Be)*

Exile leader Professor Siletski (Stanley Ridges) and Polish pilots in the RAF, with Lieutenant Stanislav Sobinski (right, Robert Stack). *(To Be or Not to Be)*

A "terribly frightened and terribly thrilled" Maria Tura (Carole Lombard) succeeds in entrancing Professor Siletski (Stanley Ridges). *(To Be or Not to Be)*

by the professor that the English have nicknamed him "Concentration Camp Erhardt," Tura responds with a hearty laugh and the remark by which the film's admirers recognize each other, "So they call me Concentration Camp Erhardt." It was Tura's next line, however, that displayed an appreciation of the Nazis' cynical cruelty on the part of Lubitsch and his writers, "We Germans do the concentrating, and the Poles do the camping." Before long Tura has the report for which the entire exercise has been arranged, but Siletski casually mentions the duplicate set he would send off to Berlin the next morning. Stalling for time, Tura asks the professor about his dinner guest, Maria Tura, and learns for the first time of his wife's affair with the young flier. Growing livid, Tura begins to threaten her and the pilot with all the powers of the Gestapo, until Siletski coolly mentions that the only one who need become upset was the husband. Within a few minutes Siletski recognizes a trap; in his rage Tura tugs on one of the false doorknobs and very soon Siletski is being hunted down by the actors in their former theater. Shot down by Sobinski, Siletski literally holds center stage as the actors stare in rapt attention at the man dying when the curtain is lifted.

The German spy's death, however, has left Maria Tura trapped in the hotel used by the Germans as a staff headquarters, a hostage until Siletski's return. Tura must assume the dead man's identity in order to rescue his wife. Wearing a false goatee and glasses, Tura arrives at the hotel room to destroy the duplicate report and free his wife, when a real SS adjutant arrives to summon him to the real Colonel Erhardt. Despite his danger, Tura can not help discussing the affair between Madame Tura and a young pilot in front of the adjutant, Captain Schultz (Henry Victor), the model of a Prussianized Nazi who neither smokes nor drinks. "Just like our Fuhrer," remarks an appropriately admiring Tura. The scenes between Tura's Siletski and Colonel Erhardt (Sig Rumann), are perhaps the most hilarious and the most controversial in the film, but are in any event the best performances either actor has ever given.

Having been prepared for the appropriate dialogue by the real Siletski, Tura confidently walks into the Nazi headquarters repeating the remark about breathing Gestapo air again and telling the real Colonel about his English nickname. When Erhardt repeats Tura's impromptu line, the actor could smile at the audience and to himself and reply, "I thought you'd say that." Erhardt is, however, a real SS man and wants the names Siletski had learned in England. Stalling for time, Tura begins to feed useless names to the inquisitive Gestapo chief, but when Erhardt summons Schultz to instigate arrests, the nervous adjutant can only say that the man had been arrested and shot, on the colonel's orders, weeks ago. Frustrated, Erhardt seeks to relieve the tension by telling Siletski a joke that has been going around Warsaw recently; the joke (about cheese being named after Hitler) leaves Tura cold. Frowning at Erhardt, the actor, who had learned the joke months before, scolds the Gestapo man for laughing at such humor. Bewildered and terrified by the charge of belittling the Führer, Erhardt pleads with Tura to remain silent, a favor Tura kindly grants. A few more names of a few more executed Poles, and Tura soon implies that Schultz is trying to pass the blame on to Erhardt. Swallowing the bait whole, Erhardt agrees and then goes on to express his misgivings about men like his adjutant who neither smoked nor drank. For the second time, Tura frowns at Erhardt and warns him about insulting the Führer. Babbling his apol-

ogies, Erhardt not only forgets about the important list of names but promises Tura a plane to take him to Berlin the next evening. On his way out, however, the colonel does manage to remember the husband of the Madame Tura about whom he had heard.

"Yes," comments Erhardt, "what he did to Shakespeare, we are now doing to Poland." This closing line, more an attack on an actor's vanity than anything else, was attacked by wartime critics as an example of Lubitsch's poor taste, a morbid joke at Poland's expense. That the line was spoken by a caricatured Nazi and was, if anything, an honest appraisal of German intentions in the occupied East was unnoticed. The film's real humor and flaw lay in the depiction of the Nazis as purely comic types, either rigid martinets like Schultz or pompous tyrants like Erhardt. Only Siletski was seen as a truly dangerous opponent, but of course he was a spy, and even he could not resist Maria Tura's charm.

Joseph Tura's success with Erhardt, however, is nearly ruined when the body of the real Siletski is discovered by German troops reopening the theater for a visit by the Führer to Warsaw. Shortly after the colonel learns of

Siletski (Stanley Ridges) greeted at the door of the phony Gestapo office by bogus German general (Lionel Atwill). *(To Be or Not to Be)*

Tura (right, Jack Benny) and Dobosh (left, Charles Halton) restrain Sobinski (Robert Stack) from rushing to shoot Siletski. *(To Be or Not to Be)*

this discovery, Tura calls to arrange his plane trip out of the occupied city. Having propped the dead man up in an armchair, the Gestapo chief then invites Tura to wait in the room, while he and his subordinates wait for Tura to crack. Fortunately, Tura has brought an extra false beard and after shaving the corpse, applies it, so that the interchange between actor and SS man was an ironic gem. In a parody of the deductive detective, Tura and Schultz trade questions and answers, while Erhardt emphatically praises his adjutant, until Tura suggests that the colonel test the dead man's goatee. The incongruity of Gestapo men behaving like Teutonic versions of Sherlock Holmes is heightened, of course, by Tura's condescension as the injured party. The actor's second great triumph, mirrored by Erhardt's growing rage at his adjutant, is destroyed, not by the Germans, but by his fellow actors. In a move to rescue Tura from a presumed trap, Kawitch, dressed as a German general, leads the disguised pack of perform-

The theatrics of dramatics: A dying Siletski (Stanley Ridges) dominates the stage. *(To Be or Not to Be)*

ers into Erhardt's office to seize Tura. Before a stunned Erhardt, Kawitch rips off Tura's own false beard and leads him away for interrogation. Ashamed and shocked, Erhardt begins to blubber when Tura turns, grinning, and reminds the colonel of the "piece of cheese."

The film's last great impersonation has the entire company, disguised as high-ranking officers, attend the celebration for Hitler's entry into Warsaw. After the ceremony begins an undisguised Greenberg (Felix Bressart), one of the bit players who had dreamed of playing Shylock, enters the corridor lined with helmeted SS men. In their surprise, the guards do not notice that from the rest room Hitler (Dugan) and his apparent staff have emerged. To the cries of "Heil" the actors manage to take Hitler's own plane, with Sobinski at the controls, out of Warsaw. Once safely in England, where Tura has always wanted to play Hamlet, there occurs the repetition of a member of the audience leaving his seat when the famed soliloquy begins. This time it is not Sobinski, notes Tura, but a young naval officer.

The final masquerade as the troupe prepares to flee Warsaw in style. From left: Dobosh (Charles Halton); (George Lynn); Bronski (Tom Dugan); Kawitch (Lionel Atwill); Tura (Jack Benny); and Sobinski (Robert Stack). *(To Be or Not to Be)*

In occupied Warsaw, the theater awaits the Führer's visit, in this use of the film's outdoor set. *(To Be or Not to Be)*

Despite its current appeal, *To Be or Not to Be* was not a success. Audiences concerned about real battles and actual casualty lists were not amused by Lubitsch's and Mayer's ironic jokes and impersonations, even at the expense of foils as familiar as Sig Rumann. The elements of serious anti-fascism, such as the last minute explosion of a rail station or Greenberg's delivery of Shylock's lines to a bogus Hitler did not fit well into the more finely wrought humor. Despite its superb parody of the German concern for hierarchy and the Nazi adulation of Hitler, the film's emphasis on the theatricality of a real war did not suit contemporary audiences. The film's most fervent fans lay among the generation born a few years after its initial release.

Other studios were not lax in producing wartime spy comedies, and one of the most successful was Paramount's *My Favorite Blonde,* starring Bob Hope and Madeleine Carroll. This was the first of three spy film comedies with the famous wisecracker playing essentially the same role, a down-at-the-heels performer forced by circumstances or higher authorities into playing the role of a spy. Basically a variant on the theme of the heroic victim, Hope's character was a sophisticated coward who often thought better of the espionage game, but carried out his assignments from a mixture of fear, if he got caught by his opponents, and love, for the leading lady, usually a real spy. Besides the slapstick provided by car chases and gunplay, Hope always reserved the right to criticize his own and others' behavior throughout the film with a series of jokes and non sequiturs.

In *My Favorite Blonde* Hope appears as Larry Haines, a vaudevillian whose current job is to act as straight man to a penguin. The animal seems to have a promising future as a film star, so Haines has to escort it to Los Angeles. Aboard the train Haines meets Karen Bentley (Madeleine Carroll), who must deliver a brooch containing vital information to a contact in the West Coast city. At the station she has noticed the two enemy agents (Lionel Royce and Victor Varconi), in the required garb of overcoats and slouch hats, on her trail. Her attempt to obtain Haines' help was a near

A shocked Colonel Erhardt (Sig Rumann) can barely salute the man whom he thinks is his Fuhrer, while Marie Tura (Carole Lombard) soon remembers it is only the bit player Bronski (Tom Dugan). *(To Be or Not to Be)*

parody of *The 39 Steps,* with a neat role reversal, particularly since Carroll was the female lead in both films. The cynical Haines is reluctant to believe her, and when she tells him about feeling watched and hounded every moment (a near satire of Hannay's impromptu campaign speech), Haines quips that he had felt that way once, but paid cash for everything now.

Even the film's basic structure, an episodic chase across country by train, car and airplane, was a parody of the adventure spy film with a very unwilling hero and a beleaguered female agent. At one point Karen rhetorically demands whether Haines is a man or a mouse, and he, following her logic, asks for a piece of cheese. Since both espionage and vaudeville depended on appearance and a cynical ability to adapt to anything, his gags complemented the spy film formulae. When Karen finally tells him that she is a British agent, the stand-up comic responds with a crisp, "Too late, sister, I've already got an agent."

The mixture of farce and adventure: mad chases, exotic women and a comic, was immensely successful. Hope appeared in two similar films, *My Favorite Brunette* and *My Favorite Spy,* after the war, while a Harold Lloyd production made in 1942 featured Kay Kyser, the band leader, as the unlikely hero. Despite their success this kind of spy film parody never dared challenge the nature of espionage, only its outer forms. In later years there

Larry Haines (Bob Hope) unsuccessfully tries to scare German agents Lanz, Karl, and Miller and Madame Runnick (left to right: Otto Reichow; Lionel Royce; Victor Varconi; and Gale Sondergaard) for the benefit of Karen Bentley (Madeleine Carroll). *(My Favorite Blonde)*

appeared a peculiar symbiosis between the comic and the exciting in the popular spy film, and it grew difficult to separate the various elements in the James Bond series or their successors. A 1960 film that did criticize the spy masters was Carol Reed's *Our Man in Havana,* from a screenplay written by the original novelist, Graham Greene.

Set in the Cuban capital "before the recent revolution," the film took that favorite screen character, the heroic victim, and added the absurdity of official self-deception. The protagonist was James Wormold (Alec Guinness), a vacuum cleaner dealer combatting poor sales and the growing costs of rearing a teenaged daughter sheltered from the corrupt Latin metropolis. Contrasted with the atmosphere of sexual provocation, crowded streets and loud music was Hawthorne (Noel Coward), a dark-suited man with bowler and umbrella who enters Wormold's shop and in be-

tween glances at the vacuum cleaner parts asks whether Wormold is "truly English." A stodgy model of espionage etiquette, Hawthorne insists on following the standardized routine of clandestine practice. Although totally conspicuous on the street, Hawthorne has Wormold meet him in the men's room of a local bar where he recruits him as British agent 59200/5, "our man in Havana." Bewildered and a little amused, Wormold accepts the honor of serving his country and being paid $150 monthly plus expenses for a monthly report—after all, his daughter Milly (Jo Morrow) wanted to own a horse, join a country club and have all the other luxuries of the wealthy in 1959 Havana.

Faced by his abject failure to recruit members of the country club as spies and worried about the punishment for accepting intelligence service funds without supplying much in the way of information, Wormold consults

Karen Bentley (Madeleine Carroll) explains Larry Haines's (Bob Hope) role in saving microfilm for its proper recipients,

Colonels Ashmont and Raeburn (Matthew Boulton and William Forrest). *(My Favorite Blonde)*

Attempting to be inconspicuous, Hawthorne (left, Noel Coward) suggests to James Wormold (Alec Guinness) that they go and talk in the men's room. *(Our Man in Havana)*

his older friend, the German expatriate, Dr. Hasselbacher (Burl Ives). Sipping drinks at their favorite bar, the two men discuss the harmlessness of inventions, so that Wormold's failures at the country club are turned into glowing reports of successful recruits and missions. Using the club's membership list, as well as pieces of gossip, Wormold constructs a network of spies and informers, all with the requisite code numbers, 59200/5, so beloved by professional and amateur spy masters. His agents include airline pilots, a professor, an engineer and even a courtesan for a cabinet minister, all of whose salaries and expenses go to Wormold.

"There is something about a secret," Hasselbacher had told Wormold, "that makes people want to believe it," and the intelligence chiefs back in London demonstrate the truth of this axiom. Blind in one eye, unaware of the exact location of the West Indies on his giant wall map, the Intelligence Chief, reputedly known only as C (Ralph Richardson), has conjured up a picture of Wormold as a merchant king developing a network of agents to rival the Americans and Russians. In a hilarious spoof of the traditional high-level briefing session, C, Hawthorne and a number of military aides played by the familiar faces of the British screen (Raymond Huntley, Maurice Denham and Hugh Manning), pore over the reports and sketches Wormold has sent. "What do you make of this?" C asks of Hawthorne, who fearing the worst, weakly mutters, "A giant vacuum cleaner, sir." Crowing with delight, C warns his staff that the odd constructions Wormold reported going up in the Cuban hills could make the hydrogen bomb obsolete. Wormold's need for money, the spy masters' desire to believe in fiendish military plans and the human inability to see the emperor's nudity conspire to give the illusion of reality to Wormold's fabrications.

The diffident vacuum cleaner salesman, however, is upset by a more immediate problem: Milly has attracted the romantic attention of Havana's secret police chief, Captain Segura (Ernie Kovacs). A cynical tyrant, who explains to Milly's father that there were classes of people whom you tortured and classes you did not, Segura is bothered by Wormold's reluctance to see his daughter in the captain's company and strange reports he has been receiving about the vacuum cleaner dealer's activities. As performed by the innovative American humorist, Kovacs, Segura was an unlikely combination of government functionary and bourgeois who laughed off Wormold's unease at being in the company of a hated policeman and yet promised the Englishman that his widow would enjoy the benefits of a Swiss bank account. Wormold's own finances were very good; he is seen depositing his monthly payments, the reward, he tells Milly, for his new endeavor, science fiction writing. Those fictions, however, had been taken seriously not only by C, who had dispatched professional helpers to Wormold, but by an unknown antagonist, as well.

While Wormold is trying to adapt himself to a trained ciphers clerk, Beatrice Bevern (Maureen O'Hara), and a radio operator, Rudy (Timothy Bateson), sent from London, Hasselbacher is being pressured into spying on his old friend. Meeting at their bar, the aging German tells Wormold that if the English intelligence service believed in his reports, other spies would too. In the minds of the spy masters, the difference between truth and falsehood was merely a matter of choice and whim, and Wormold's lies soon became more dangerous than the truth. The film's tone changes drastically after Hasselbacher invites Wormold and Beatrice to view his wrecked laboratory, the price for his refusal to spy on Wormold. To underline the growing danger, Wormold also learns that the Cuban airlines pilot he had recruited from the club's roster had died in a car crash, shortly after he had reported to London that the pilot had died in a fictitious plan crash near those mysterious constructions in the hills. Like a poet gifted with fearful powers of prophecy, Wormold's inventions have taken on life and are dealing out death.

Wormold (Alec Guinness) shows his daughter, Milly (Jo Morrow), the sketches for his "science-fiction" stories. *(Our Man in Havana)*

Wormold (Alec Guinness) dictates a message concerning the death of one of his "agents" to Beatrice Bevern (Maureen O'Hara). *(Our Man in Havana)*

Captain Segura (Ernie Kovacs) incredulously notes the pieces with which Wormold (left, Alec Guinness) intends to play checkers. *(Our Man in Havana)*

The man's dilemma is heightened by the growing affection with which Beatrice urges him to make use of his other agents, since the situation has grown dangerous. A faint, sad smile playing around his features, Wormold dismisses her suggestion with the fact that it was his duty, not that of his subordinates, to face any potential threat. Wormold is soon told that the potential is real, since an enemy agent has been ordered to kill him at an impending businessmen's luncheon. Sitting comfortably beneath a palm tree, Hawthorne tells Wormold that he had been frankly suspicious of the drawings, since they resembled vacuum cleaner parts, but that this move by the opposition definitely confirmed his reports. Unassuming and placid, Wormold was in the absurdist position of having people believe in him so much that his own life was endangered, and that fact, of itself, had raised his value in the eyes of people like Hawthorne. The baneful side of the semicomic intrigue was soon found lying near his favorite bar; Dr. Hasselbacher was murdered.

The film's first death prompts Wormold

Dr. Hasselbacher (left, Burl Ives) shows Wormold (Alec Guinness) his wrecked apartment. *(Our Man in Havana)*

Rival vacuum cleaner dealer and spy, Hubert Carter (Paul Rogers), takes a shot at Wormold in front of brothel door. *(Our Man in Havana)*

to tell Beatrice the truth about his reports and spies, a truth she laughingly accepts, since she too has grown embittered over her inability to face the lethal side of her profession. There is, however, still the problem of Segura's courtship of Milly and the nameless, faceless assassin of whom the only trace is a stutter on a tape recorded phone conversation with Hasselbacher. At the business lunch, Wormold and the other guests switch plates in an effort to avoid disliked vegetables, while the terrified look of a nearby waiter hints at something more dangerous than underdone carrots. By a lucky accident, a spilled drink and a thirsty dog, Wormold learns that his would-be murderer is not only another Englishman, but also a nondescript salesman from a rival vacuum cleaner firm, Hubert Carter (Paul Rogers). Aware of his foe and determined to leave Havana with Milly, Wormold takes it upon himself not only to deal with Carter, but to end Segura's courtship, too.

Accepting Segura's bid for Milly's hand in marriage, Wormold makes the engagement the stakes in a checkers match with the police captain, but with a collection of miniature whiskey bottles in place of the traditional pieces. Every bottle taken must be drunk by its winner, and so Segura, who has been winning

the game, soon collapses in a drunken stupor, while Wormold takes his pistol and ventures out for a prearranged night on the town with Carter. Contrasted with Wormold's calm ease, Carter is nervous and grows increasingly agitated when he realizes that Wormold is taking him to a different bar from the one they had discussed. From one sleazy bar to another, Wormold can see Carter's growing fear and even comments on his discomfort in front of a stripper at one night club. Leaving him in front of a brothel, Wormold has decided to let the man live; after all, Carter had protested, "We're only soldiers who follow orders, you and I." But after Carter's potshot at his back, Wormold shoots him down. Carter's death signifies the end of his assignment as 59200/5 and his life in Havana; he and Milly are ordered to leave by a Segura who stares in disbelief at the apparently ineffectual little man.

Back in London, Wormold, with Beatrice hanging on his arm, awaits the verdict of C, Hawthorne and the military advisors, all of whom blame each other for having taken the drawings seriously. Rather than admit their error by prosecuting Wormold, C offers him an Order of the British Empire and a permanent post on the teaching staff to train new agents in the handling of district offices. Wormold's imagination is rewarded in another way as well: in the film's final scene, the former spy stares in amused revelation at the toys being sold by a street vendor. The toy is a motorized scale model of the inventions he had pictured in the Cuban mountains.

Our Man in Havana was an ambitious production; besides featuring performances by a number of gifted, if ill-matched, actors, it tried to say something ultimately serious about espionage within the outlines of a witty comedy. Spies, the film noted, were often like anybody else, so that the only real difference between Wormold and Carter was that the latter was willing to have someone killed because of his orders. The spy masters, C and Hawthorne, were depicted as caricatures, but their decisions had helped kill Hasselbacher, may have meant the death of an innocent pilot, and nearly resulted in Wormold's murder. Since a secret and a secret agent needed only enough people to believe in them, the illusion of intrigue was all that was necessary, and that became the core of a 1973 French film, *The Tall Blonde Man with One Black Shoe.*

Unlike the Carol Reed film, this Yves Robert production was a popular success in France and was the first spy film comedy to achieve some success among American audiences in years. Rather than a heroic victim fooling the spy chiefs, this import had a fool turned into a hero despite the spy chiefs' own intentions. The film opens conventionally enough with a man wired to a battery of lie detectors facing an interrogation by New York City detectives. Charged with smuggling heroin, the man pleads that he is carrying out a special assignment for the head of French Counter-Intelligence. That man (Jean Rochefort), however, knows nothing about "such filthy business" and suspects a conspiracy to defame him by his own subordinate, Milan (Bernard Blier). To snare Milan, the French spy master decides to throw him a piece of cheese around which its victim would construct an elaborate trap. Knowing full well that Milan has wiretaps in his office, the counter-intelligence chief tells his assistant, Perruche, that an important agent is soon to arrive by plane. The assistant has orders to pick anybody at random, and so the lanky concert violinist, Francois Perrin (Pierre Richard), soon becomes the center of attention for Milan's army of spies.

Directed by Yves Robert from a screenplay co-authored with Francis Veber, the film took advantage of all the visual clichés of the spy film adventure. Photographed from all sides, the screen was full of the frame-freezed shots of Perrin's facial contortions as he chewed a candy. When he leaves for a dental appointment, a dozen agents enter his apartment and without a single word of dialogue go through the expertly choreographed examination of Perrin's belongings. The musician, however, is too unpredictable for the spies. Frantically calling their colleagues by radiotelephone, the men assigned to follow Perrin are shocked to see him going to the park rather than the dentist. In another sequence borowed from the traditional canon of espionage films, Milan reviews the life and career of Perrin in a slide show presentation of all his Baptismal, school and army records. The man's "perfectly normal life" only spurs Milan to increase his efforts to discover the nonexistent secret. The only secret Perrin does have is purely domestic: he is having an affair with his friend's wife, all three of them members of the same orchestra. This revelation does not help Milan, of course, so he resorts to the feminine

Captain Segura (right, Ernie Kovacs) bids James and Milly Wormold (Alec Guinness and Jo Morrow) farewell from Havana. *(Our Man in Havana)*

Pierre Richard as the violinist Francois Perrin in this publicity still from *The Tall Blond Man with One Black Shoe.*

lure. One of his agents (Mireille Darc) is assigned to seduce Perrin and for the event she wears a clinging, black, three-quarters dress—there wasn't much of it from her nape to her lower spine.

Seated formally in evening dress, Milan, his lieutenants and their wives watch the attempted seduction on a closed circuit television set. Torn between their interest in the sexual misadventure and their amazement at Perrin's clumsiness, the men would lean forward at the mere mention of a potential secret, only to fall back in their seats when Perrin's great secret is revealed, his desire to compose. Realizing that the man is either too professional to break or a mere fool without importance, Milan orders him dispatched. As Milan's men follow him, blackjacks at the ready, the camera, in a long shot from behind, reveals that Milan's men themselves are being

Mireille Darc as Christine, latter-day Mata Hari, in "that dress" from *The Tall Blond Man with One Black Shoe.*

followed, so that Perrin continues unaware of the two unconscious men being carried off behind his back.

That was the film's essential joke, that while a complete innocent, an angelic fool was being filmed, watched and tape recorded in a futile search for information, the spies following him were themselves being filmed, watched and listed for proscription. The French spy master could even comment on the inordinate number of agents Milan employed. Having chronicled Milan's treachery, his superior demands an end to the farce and decides to call off the violinist's bodyguards, but the assistant, Perruche, who has watched with amused approval the musician's antics, gives the guards the exact opposite orders. Ambush is met by counter-ambush as one pair of assassins run into another pair in Perrin's apartment. While the silencer-equipped automatics sputter, the only witness is a bewildered, cuckolded husband who becomes more and more distracted as the bodies he has seen lying on the floor disappear every time Perrin

Colonel Milan (Bernard Blier) has the drop on an already distraught Maurice (Jean Carmel). *(The Tall Blond Man with One Black Shoe)*

looks. The men of French counter-intelligence manage to be as competent housekeepers as they are guardians.

At the film's close the musician is seen flying off to Rio de Janeiro with an oversized steamer trunk containing the beautiful blonde agent with whom he has fallen in love. The only two hints of complexity were the voice of the spy master pompously declaring that the young man seemed to have potential as a new recruit, and the inter-title that French law guaranteed the inviolability of private life. The heroic fool has had a long tradition in folk tale and literature, so that his emergence in the spy film was nearly predictable. Chosen by whim because of his mismatched shoes, the angelically oblivious character earned not only the love of a professional spy, but the important help of the spy chief's aide and that man's grudging admiration, as well. To avoid the lethal dangers of espionage, particularly as dealt out by one's own government, only blind chance, good luck and soulful innocence

could help. This idea, reinforced in recent years by the complexities of real espionage and actual foreign relations, seemed to find millions of supporters among French film audiences. Not only was there *The Return of the Tall Blonde Man with One Black Shoe,* but in 1975 another good-natured simpleton was unleashed on another evildoer, and was appropriately titled *A Pain in the A**.*

A professional assassin (Lino Ventura), the titular antagonist, opens the film. Equally adept and remorseless about using either time bombs or rifle, he is a hard-boiled, violent fellow from whom bigger men back away at bars. Assigned to kill an important government witness on the morning of his testimony, the killer books a room in an ornate hotel overlooking the law court and the lines of policemen assigned to guard it. Lurking in a nearby room, however, is the film's protagonist, the killer's nemesis (Jacques Brel), a good-natured salesman lamenting for his estranged wife. While the murderer goes through the semi-

The Assassin (right, Lino Ventura) casts the first of many grimaces at the Boob (Jacques Brel), in *A Pain in the A***.

ritualistic, precise movements for setting up his sniper rifle, the salesman is preparing a noose for himself. Adjusting the cross-hairs of his scope, the professional gunman soon hears the sound of rushing water and the commotion of people in the hallway in front of his room. In a furious effort to end this distraction and threat to his security, the killer crashes into the salesman's room to discover the semi-conscious man with a rope around his neck and a broken water line the cause for all the commotion. The killer has also found a new lifelong friend, as the salesman gleefully begins to recount his life and unhappiness.

As directed by Edouard Molinaro, *A Pain in the A*** episodically chronicles each of the futile efforts by which the killer tries to rid himself of a man who has the affectionate, clinging power of a moonstruck puppy. The unlikely pair were a parody of the cinematically traditional male friendship cliché, since every event only thrust the two together again. Even the unsuccessful assassination attempt is seen by the grinning pal as a spur to increased loyalty, so that the would-be killer is pursued not only by the police, but by his idiotic friend as well. In the film's closing frame-freeze, the cool professional, in striped prison garb, can only throw an agonized look of hatred at his fellow inmate, his pal, who gleefully tells him that he has arranged a transfer into the same cell. The film's implication was that a fool's luck was more than a match for anyone.

All the spy film comedies took the logic of espionage to its logical conclusion—that the difference between truth and falsehood, appearance and reality, "cover" and mission was an article of faith, a shared illusion. From the Warsaw stage to the actual Gestapo headquarters was merely a matter of accents and a false goatee, and between Wormold's fictions and the planning of the spy masters, a question of belief. Since the reasons for spies and counter-spies, the state's vaunted security, were made up by spies in the first place, espionage had become a modern joke on the world scale and the best remedy was to play the fool.

Conclusions

Spying, whether absurd or murderous, was a rotten, dirty business. This was the truth about espionage as depicted in the films about it, but there was another facet, as well—the awful necessity for intelligence and counter-intelligence. There were real spies in the world, and except for the outright comedies, no one has ever denied their efficacy or need. Whether politically motivated or romantically inspired, both Kurt Muller and Rick Blaine chose to become spies for a specific cause in a historic time. They, however, were amateurs, and the professionals have come to dominate espionage since the end of the last war. Even the harmless, well-meaning Wormold had to kill to save his own life, and the innocent Perrin was appraised in professional terms by the spy master who had tacitly condemned him. The army officers who sent the idealistic Luftwaffe medic, Happy, off to his death have their equals in the offices of every major espionage organization, and a few minor ones, as well. The London officials who plotted Fiedler's death were served by men like Mundt who had survived two rival dictatorships. Professionalism had replaced the amateur idealism of the earlier films; the double-agent Cross was a more typical character than either Hannay or Ashenden.

With expertise and neutrality came the studied avoidance of causes and goals, save that of a job well done, whatever its effects. The task of protecting what used to be called the Free World had already grown dim by the early 1960's, when James Bond supplied a novel set of incentives for engaging in espionage. That cruel symbol of East–West hostility, the Berlin Wall, became the visual metaphor for the amorality of the espionage war that claimed innocent, as well as tainted, lives. The ambiguity surrounding government spying against government was compounded by indications that the spies, assassins and thugs could be unleashed against fellow citizens even more easily than against foreign agents. It did not seem to matter to the spy masters against whom their talents and energies were aimed. In an almost cyclical progression, from *Spies* to *The Parallax View,* spy films have returned to the elaborate adversary dramas of the twenties, when mysterious forces changed society and faceless agents murdered officials before the eyes of that ultimate innocent bystander, the public. But unlike the Fritz Lang classic, the villainous spy master was never seen, let alone caught.

Filmography

A Sense of Adventure

SPIES (SPIONE) Producer-director, Fritz Lang; UFA Studio (Germany), 1927–28; with: Rudolph Klein-Rogge, Gerda Maurus, Willy Fritsch, Lupu Pick, Fritz Rasp and Lien Deyers.

THE SCARLET PIMPERNEL Producer, Alexander Korda; Director, Harold Young; United Artists, 1935; with: Leslie Howard, Merle Oberon, Raymond Massey, Joan Gardner, Walter Rilla, John Turnbull and Nigel Bruce.

THE 39 STEPS Producer, Michael Balcon; Director, Alfred Hitchcock; General Films Distributors (Great Britain), 1935; with: Robert Donat, Madeleine Carroll, Lucie Mannheim, Godfrey Tearle, Peggy Ashcroft, John Laurie and Frank Cellier.

STATE SECRET (THE GREAT MANHUNT) Produced and directed by Sidney Gilliat and Frank Launder; Columbia, 1950; with: Douglas Fairbanks, Jr., Jack Hawkins, Glynis Johns, Herbert Lom, Karel Stepanek, Walter Rilla and Anton Diffring.

DR. NO Produced by Harry Saltzman and Albert Broccoli; Director, Terence Young; United Artists, 1963; with: Sean Connery, Ursula Andress, Joseph Wiseman, Jack Lord, Bernard Lee, Anthony Dawson, Lois Maxwell, John Kitzmiller, Zena Marshall, Eunice Gayson, and Yvonne Shima.

THE IPCRESS FILE Producer, Harry Saltzman; Director, Sidney Furie; Universal, 1965; with: Michael Caine, Nigel Green, Guy Doleman, Sue Lloyd, Gordon Jackson, Frank Gatliff and Oliver MacGreevy.

A Feel for Politics

WATCH ON THE RHINE Producer, Hal Wallis; Director, Herman Shumlin; Warner Bros., 1943; with: Paul Lukas, George Coulouris, Bette Davis, Lucile Watson, Geraldine Fitzgerald, Donald Woods, Henry Daniell, Eric Roberts, Donald Woods, Kurt Katch and Janis Wilson.

THE IRON CURTAIN Producer, Sol Siegel; Director, William Wellman; 20th Century-Fox, 1948; with: Dana Andrews, Gene Tierney, June Havoc, Stefan Schnabel, Barry Kroeger, Eduard Franz, Frederick Tozere, Edna Best, Leslie Barrie, Noel Cravat, Victor Wood and Reed Hadley.

WALK EAST ON BEACON Producer, Louis de Rochemont; Director, Alfred Werker; Columbia, 1952; with: George Murphy, Finlay Currie, Virginia Gilmore, Karel Stepanek, Bruno Wick, Ernest Graves and Louisa Horton, Peter Capell, Karl Weber, Rev. Robert Dunn and Jack Manning.

MY SON JOHN Producer-director, Leo McCarey; Paramount, 1952; with: Helen Hayes, Van Heflin, Robert Walker, Dean Jagger, Minor Watson, Frank McHugh, Richard Jaeckel, James Young, Irene Winston and Todd Karns.

NORTH BY NORTHWEST Produced and directed by Alfred Hitchcock; Metro-Goldwyn-Mayer, 1959; with: Cary Grant, James Mason, Eva Marie Saint, Martin Landau, Leo G. Carroll, Adam Williams, Robert Ellenstein, Jessie Royce Landis, Philip Ober, Josephine Hutchinson and Edward Platt.

THE SPY WHO CAME IN FROM THE COLD Produced and directed by Martin Ritt; Paramount, 1965; with: Richard Burton, Claire Bloom, Oskar Werner, Peter Van Eyck, Sam Wanamaker, George Voskovec, Rupert Davies, Cyril Cusack, Michael Hordern, Bernard Lee and Walter Gotel.

LA GUERRE EST FINIE Director, Alain Resnais; Sofracima-Europa-Film (France-Sweden), 1967; with: Yves Montand, Ingrid Thulin, Genevieve Bujold, Jean Daste, Paul Crauchet, Michel Piccoli, Jean Bouise, Jacques Rispal, R.J. Chauffar, Jose-Maria Flotats, and Roland Monod.

EXECUTIVE ACTION Producer, Edward Lewis; Director, David Miller; National General, 1974; with: Robert Ryan, Burt Lancaster, Will Geer, Ed Lauter, Richard Bell and Lee Delano.

The Problem of Loyalty

THE ADVENTURESS (British title: I SEE A DARK STRAN-

GER) Produced and directed by Frank Launder; General Films Distributors (Great Britain), 1947; with: Deborah Kerr, Trevor Howard, Raymond Huntley, David Ward, Katie Johnson, Harry Hutchinson, Norman Shelley, Garry Marsh, Tom Macaulay, and James Harcourt.

DECISION BEFORE DAWN   Produced and directed by Anatole Litvak, 20th Century-Fox, 1952; with: Richard Basehart, Oskar Werner, Gary Merrill, Hildegarde Neff, O.E. Hasse, Hans Christian Blech, Dominique Blanchar, Wilfried Seyfert, Helene Thimig and Klaus Kinski.

THE DEADLY AFFAIR   Produced and directed by Sidney Lumet; Columbia, 1966; with: James Mason, Simone Signoret, Maximilian Schell, Harriet Andersson, Harry Andrews, Kenneth Haigh, Roy Kinnear and Max Andrian.

SCORPIO   Producer, Walter Mirisch; Director, Michael Winner; United Artists, 1973; with: Burt Lancaster, Paul Scofield, Gayle Hunnicut, Alain Delon, Shmul Rodensky, Vladek Sheybal, John Colicos, J.D. Cannon, Joanne Linville, Melvin Stewart, Sandoe Eles and Frederick Jaeger.

THREE DAYS OF THE CONDOR   Producer, Stanley Schneider; Director, Sidney Pollack; Paramount, 1974; with: Robert Redford, Faye Dunaway, Cliff Robertson, John Houseman, Max Von Sydow, Tina Chen, Michael Kane, Hank Garret and Jay Devlin.

The Possibility of War

THE LADY VANISHES   Producer, Edward Black; Director, Alfred Hitchcock; Gaumont (Great Britain), 1938; with: Margaret Lockwood, Michael Redgrave, Paul Lukas, Dame May Whitty, Cecil Parker, Mary Clare, Basil Radford, Naunton Wayne, Linden Travers, and Catharine Lacey.

CONFESSIONS OF A NAZI SPY   Produced and directed by Anatole Litvak; Warner Bros., 1939; with: Edward G. Robinson, Francis Lederer, George Sanders, Paul Lukas, Henry O'Neill, Sig Rumann, Dorothy Tree, Lya Lys, Hans von Twardowsky, James Stephenson and Martin Kosleck.

FOREIGN CORRESPONDENT   Producer, Walter Wanger; Director, Alfred Hitchcock; United Artists, 1940; with: Joel McCrea, Laraine Day, George Sanders, Herbert Marshall, Albert Bassermann, Eduardo Ciannalli, Edmund Gwenn, Harry Davenport, Robert Benchley, and Martin Kosleck.

ACROSS THE PACIFIC   Producer, Jerry Wald; Director, John Huston; Warner Bros., 1942; with: Humphrey Bogart, Mary Astor, Sydney Greenstreet, Frank Wilcox, Monte Blue, Richard Loo and Charles Halton.

THE INVADERS (British title: THE 49th PARALLEL) Produced and directed by Michael Powell; Columbia, 1942; with: Eric Portman, Leslie Howard, Raymond Massey, Laurence Olivier, Anton Walbrook, Finlay Currie, Glynis Johns, Ley On, Niall MacGinnis, Raymond Lovell, Charles Victor, John Chandos and Basil Appleby.

THE HOUSE ON 92nd STREET   Producer, Louis de Rochemont; Director, Henry Hathaway; 20th Century-Fox, 1945; with: Lloyd Nolan, Signe Hasso, Leo G. Carroll, William Eythe, Gene Lockhart, Bruno Wick, Harro Meller, Alfred Lindner, Lydia St. Clair, and Charles Wagenheim.

The Intricacies of War

THE SPY IN BLACK (alternative title: U-29)   Produced and directed by Michael Powell; Columbia, 1939; with: Conrad Veidt, Valerie Hobson, Sebastian Shaw, Marius Goring, June Duprez, and Cyril Raymond.

FIVE GRAVES TO CAIRO   Produced and directed by Billy Wilder; Paramount, 1943; with: Franchot Tone, Anne Baxter, Akim Tamiroff, Erich von Stroheim, Peter Van Eyck, Miles Mander and Fortunio Bonanova.

CLOAK AND DAGGER   Producer, Milton Sperling; Director, Fritz Lang; Warner Bros., 1946; with: Gary Cooper, Lilli Palmer, Robert Alda, Vladimir Sokoloff, J. Edward Bromberg, Helene Thimig, Dan Seymour, Marjorie Hoshelle, Ludwig Stossel, Marc Lawrence and James Flavin.

13 RUE MADELEINE   Producer, Louis de Rochemont; Director, Henry Hathaway; 20th Century-Fox, 1946; with: James Cagney, Richard Conte, Annabella, Frank Latimore, Walter Abel, Sam Jaffe, Alfred Lindner, E.G. Marshall, Melville Cooper, Marcel Rousseau and Blanche Yurka.

THE MAN WHO NEVER WAS   Producer, Andre Hakim; Director, Ronald Neame; 20th Century-Fox, 1956; with: Clifton Webb, Gloria Grahame, Robert Flemyng, Josephine Griffin, Stephen Boyd, Andre Morell, Michael Hordern, Cyril Cusack, Laurence Naismith and Geoffrey Keen.

THE COUNTERFEIT TRAITOR   Producer, William Perlberg; Director, George Seaton; Paramount, 1961; with: William Holden, Lilli Palmer, Hugh Griffith, Eva Dahlbeck, Carl Raddatz, Ulf Palme, Stefan Schnabel, Helo Gutschwager, Ernst Schroder, Wolfgang Preiss and Erica Beer.

A Touch of Romance

DISHONORED   Produced and directed by Josef von Sternberg; Paramount, 1931; with: Marlene Dietrich, Victor McLaglen, Gustav von Seyffertitz, Warner Oland, Barry Norton and Lew Cody.

MATA HARI   Produced and directed by George Fitzmaurice; Metro-Goldwyn-Mayer, 1932; with: Greta Garbo, Ramon Novarro, Lewis Stone, Lionel Barrymore, C. Henry Gordon, Karen Morley, Alec B. Francis and Blanche Frederici.

SECRET AGENT   Producer, Michael Balcon; Director, Alfred Hitchcock; Gaumont (Great Britain), 1936; with: Madeleine Carroll, Peter Lorre, John Gielgud, Robert Young, Percy Marmont, Florence Kahn and Lilli Palmer.

NIGHT TRAIN (British title: NIGHT TRAIN TO MUNICH)   Producer, Edward Black; Director, Carol Reed; 20th Century-Fox, 1940; with: Rex Harrison, Margaret Lockwood, Paul Henreid, James Harcourt, Basil Radford, Naunton Wayne, Raymond Huntley, Felix Aylmer, Kenneth Kent and C.V. France.

CASABLANCA   Producer, Hal Wallis; Director, Michael Curtiz; Warner Bros., 1942; with: Humphrey Bogart, Ingrid Bergman, Paul Henreid, Claude Rains, Conrad Veidt, Peter Lorre, Sydney Greenstreet, Dooley Wilson, S.Z. Sakall, Leonid Kinsky, Marcel Dalio and Ludwig Stossel.

NOTORIOUS   Produced and directed by Alfred Hitchcock; RKO, 1946; with: Cary Grant, Ingrid Bergman, Claude Rains, Ivan Triesault, Madame Sebastian, Louis Calhern, Reinhold Schunzel, and Alex Minotis.

GOLDEN EARRINGS   Producer, Harry Tugend; Director, Mitchell Leisen; Paramount, 1947; with: Marlene Dietrich, Ray Milland, Murvyn Vye, Bruce Lester, Dennis Hoey, Ivan Triesault, Reinhold Schunzel and Quentin Reynolds.

The Edge of Paranoia

THE MINISTRY OF FEAR   Producer, Seton Miller; Director, Fritz Lang; Paramount, 1944; with: Ray Milland, Marjorie Reynolds, Carl Esmond, Dan Duryea, Alan Napier, Mary Field, Hillary Brooke, Percy Waram and Erskine Sanford.

THE MANCHURIAN CANDIDATE   Producer, George Axelrod; Co-producer and Director, John Frankenheimer; United Artists, 1962; with: Frank Sinatra, Laurence Harvey, Janet Leigh, Angela Lansbury, John McGiver, Khigh Dhiegh, Henry Silva, James Gregory and Leslie Parrish.

THE QUILLER MEMORANDUM   Producer, Ivan Foxwell; Director, Michael Anderson; 20th Century-Fox, 1966; with: George Segal, Alec Guinness, Senta Berger, Max Von Sydow, George Sanders, Robert Flemyng, Robert Helpmann, Peter Carsten, Edith Schneider, Gunter Meisner and Robert Stass.

THE PARALLAX VIEW   Produced and directed by Alan Pakula; Paramount, 1974; with: Warren Beatty, Paula Prentiss, Hume Cronyn, Kelly Thordsen, William Daniels, Bill Jordan, Anthony Zerbe, Kenneth Mars and Walter McGinn.

ESCAPE TO NOWHERE (*LE SILENCIEUX*)   Producer, Alain Poire; Director, Claude Pinotheau; Gaumont International, 1974; with: Lino Ventura, Leo Genn and Suzanne Flon.

LE SECRET   Produced and directed by Robert Enrico; Distributed by Cinema National, 1975; with: Jean-Louis Trintignant, Philippe Noiret, and Marlene Jobert.

The Urge for Humor

ALL THROUGH THE NIGHT   Producer, Jerry Wald; Director, Vincent Sherman; Warner Bros., 1942; with: Humphrey Bogart, Conrad Veidt, Peter Lorre, Karen Verne, Jane Darwell, Judith Anderson, Frank McHugh and William Demarest.

TO BE OR NOT TO BE   Producer, Alexander Korda; Director, Ernst Lubitsch; United Artists, 1942; with: Carole Lombard, Jack Benny, Robert Stack, Sig Rumann, Stanley Ridges, Felix Bressart, Lionel Atwill, Henry Victor, Tom Dugan, Charles Halton, Miles Mander, George Lyn and Maude Eburne.

MY FAVORITE BLONDE   Producer, Paul Jones; Director, Sidney Lanfield; Paramount, 1942; with: Bob Hope, Madeleine Carroll, Gale Sondergaard, George Zucco, Lionel Royce, Victor Varconi and Otto Reichow.

OUR MAN IN HAVANA   Producer, Raymond Anzarut; Director, Carol Reed; Columbia, 1960; with: Alec Guinness, Maureen O'Hara, Burl Ives, Ernie Kovacs, Noel Coward, Ralph Richardson, Jo Morrow, Paul Rogers, Gregoire Aslan, Maxine Audley, Timothy Bateson and Raymond Huntley.

THE TALL BLOND MAN WITH ONE BLACK SHOE   Produced and directed by Yves Robert; Released in U.S. by Cinema V, 1973; with: Pierre Richard, Jean Rochefort, Jean Carmel, Bernard Blier, Mireille Darc and Colette Castel.

A PAIN IN THE A** (*LE MERDDEUR*)   Producer, Georges Dancigers; Director, Edouard Molinaro; Released in U.S. through Corwin-Mahler, 1975; with: Lino Ventura and Jacques Brel.

3 Films Mentioned Briefly in Text

PIMPERNEL SMITH   Produced and directed by Leslie Howard; United Artists, 1941; with: Leslie Howard, Francis L. Sullivan, Mary Morris, Hugh McDermott, Raymond Huntley, Basil Appleby, Philip Friend and David Tomlinson.

PICKUP ON SOUTH STREET   Producer, Jules Schermer; Director, Samuel Fuller; 20th Century-Fox, 1953; with: Richard Widmark, Jean Peters, Thelma Ritter, Richard Kiley, Murvyn Vye, Virginia Carroll and Roger Moore.

THE KILLER ELITE   Producer, Arthur Lewis; Director, Sam Peckinpah; United Artists, 1975; with: James Caan, Robert Duvall, Arthur Hill, and Gig Young.